Phi sophy, Ris
Spo ts

General interest in adventure sports and leisure activities in which 'risk' is unavoidable grows year on year. While many such activities provide a sense of closeness to nature and heighten our awareness of the unpredictability of the outdoors, they typically require the participant to put themselves at genuine risk of injury or even death. The time is ripe for a critical and reflective assessment of this phenomenon from rigorous philosophical perspectives.

This collection of essays is the first single-source treatment of adventure sports from an exclusively philosophical standpoint, offering students a uniquely focused reader of this burgeoning area of interest as well as providing graduates and academics with a groundbreaking new direction for study in this area.

Featuring contributions from philosophers who each also have personal familiarity of participation in adventure and extreme sports, and with reference to key modern philosophers including Heidegger, Nietzsche and Kant, *Philosophy, Risk and Adventure Sports* should become a classic analysis of the intersections between philosophy and extreme experiences, encompassing essential related concepts of elation, danger, death, wilderness and authenticity.

With contributions from John Michael Atherton, Douglas Anderson, Paul Beedie, Gunnar Breivik, Alan P. Dougherty, Jesús Ilundáin-Agurruza, Ivo Jirásek, Kevin Krein, Sigmund Loland, Mike McNamee, Verner Møller, Robert E. Rinehart, Philip Ebert and Simon Robertson.

Mike McNamee is Reader in Philosophy at the Centre for Philosophy, Humanities and Law in Health Care at the University of Wales, Swansea. He is also co-editor of the Routledge book series *Ethics and Sport* and editor of the journal *Sport, Ethics and Philosophy*.

Philosophy, Risk and Adventure Sports

Edited by Mike McNamee

 Routledge
Taylor & Francis Group

LONDON AND NEW YORK

First published 2007
by Routledge
2 Park Square, Milton Park, Abingdon, Oxon OX14 4RN

Simultaneously published in the USA and Canada
by Routledge
270 Madison Ave, New York, NY 10016

Routledge is an imprint of the Taylor & Francis Group, an informa business

Typeset in Goudy
by Keystroke, 28 High Street, Tettenhall, Wolverhampton
Printed and bound in Great Britain
by Antony Rowe Ltd, Chippenham, Wiltshire

British Library Cataloguing in Publication Data
A catalogue record for this book is available from the British Library

Library of Congress Cataloging in Publication Data
Philosophy, risk and adventure sports / [edited by] Mike McNamee.
    p. cm.
    1. Outdoor recreation. 2. Extreme sports. 3. Sports–Philosophy.
I. McNamee, M. J. (Mike J.)
    GV191.6.P55 2007
    796.5–dc22
    2006039169

ISBN10: 0–415–35184–7 (hbk)
ISBN10: 0–415–35185–5 (pbk)
ISBN10: 0–203–69857–6 (ebk)

ISBN13: 978–0–415–35184–3 (hbk)
ISBN13: 978–0–415–35185–0 (pbk)
ISBN13: 978–0–203–69857–0 (ebk)

Contents

Figures

Contributors

Douglas Anderson is Professor of Philosophy at Southern Illinois University, Carbondale. He focuses on American philosophy and the history of philosophy, and is author of three books and numerous essays dealing with issues in American philosophy and culture.

John (Michael) Atherton teaches philosophy at Seton Hill University in southwest Pennsylvania, USA, where he integrates outdoor activities such as sailing, cross-country skiing, snorkelling, mountain biking, orienteering and canoeing with philosophy. His students reflect on the real consequences, unpredictability and reciprocity as they engage in kinaesthetic activity in the outdoors and do so in light of their philosophy readings.

Paul Beedie is Senior Lecturer in Sociology at De Montfort University, Bedford, where he specialises in teaching theoretical approaches to adventure recreation. He has taught, presented and written on a social analysis of adventure, on topics ranging from risk assessment to adventure tourism. He is an accomplished mountaineer with experience of wild places throughout the world. He is a member of both the Climbers' Club and the Association of Mountaineering Instructors.

Gunnar Breivik is former Rector and Professor of Social Sciences at the Norwegian University of Sport and Physical Education in Oslo where he also leads the outdoor education section. He has experience of most risk sports and is a qualified instructor of skiing, glacier walking, white-water kayaking and climbing. He has taught, lectured and published research articles on topics like 'sensation seeking', 'risk taking' and 'risk sports'.

Alan P. Dougherty is a post-graduate research student within the Institute for Environment, Philosophy and Public Policy at Lancaster University. His research interests centre on the aesthetics and ethics of upland land use and he convenes the Lancaster University Uplands Research Group. A mountaineer of some thirty-five years, he has climbed rock and ice in a variety of locations, ascended new routes and contributed to climbing guide books. Previously an active caver, and a qualified caving instructor, he has descended several of the world's deepest systems. Currently he is attempting to pursue the perfect Telemark turn whilst ski-mountaineering.

Philip Ebert completed his PhD in philosophy at the University of St Andrews, Scotland, in 2005 and is currently a Leverhulme funded Post-Doctoral Researcher at the Arché Centre at the University of St Andrews. His main philosophical research lies in epistemology and the philosophy of mathematics and logic. Outside philosophy, Philip's main interests are rock climbing, mountaineering and skiing.

Jesús Ilundáin-Agurruza lectures in philosophy at the University of New Mexico-Los Alamos. His primary areas of research and publication are in the philosophy of sport, aesthetics and the philosophy of literature. He is an avid road cyclist who races at the elite level, and is currently learning Western martial arts, including sword fighting. He used to run with the bulls until he realized that the bulls were getting too fast for him.

Ivo Jirásek is an Assistant Professor in the Faculty of Physical Culture at Palacky University Olomouc, Czech Republic. He lectures on philosophy of physical culture, ethics, religion and science. He is interested in philosophical aspects of physical culture (game and play, experience, body, movement) in experiential education. He is a consultant and chief instructor for Outward Bound – The Czech Way.

Kevin Krein is an Assistant Professor of Philosophy and the Director of Outdoor Studies at the University of Alaska Southeast. His work includes teaching and writing on philosophy of nature, philosophy of the environment and philosophy of mind. He also teaches outdoor skills courses in backcountry skiing and snowboarding, and in wilderness travel. He has extensive experience of alpine climbing, ski mountaineering and helicopter skiing and has completed several first ski descents, a winter crossing of the Juneau Icefield and a ski descent of Denali.

Sigmund Loland is Professor of Sport Philosophy at the Norwegian University of Sport and Physical Education and a past President of the International Association for the Philosophy of Sport. His book, *Fair Play*, was published by Routledge in 2002. He is a former international alpine skier and coach. He is now a keen snowboarder.

Mike McNamee is Reader in Philosophy, at the Centre for Philosophy, Humanities and Law in Healthcare, School of Health Science, University of Wales, Swansea. His research interests are in the philosophies of education, health, leisure and sport, and especially in the ethics of medicine, research and sport. He has recently co-authored *Research Ethics in Exercise, Health and Sport Sciences* (with S. Olivier and P. Wainwright, Routledge, 2006). His edited and co-edited books include *Philosophy and the Sciences of Exercise, Health and Sport* (Routledge, 2005), *Ethics and Educational Research* (with D. Bridges, Blackwell, 2002); *Ethics and Sport* (with J. Parry, Routledge, 1998) and he co-edits (with J. Parry) the book series *Ethics and Sport*. He is editor of the new journal *Sport, Ethics and Philosophy* (Routledge, 2007) and is a former President of the International Association for the Philosophy of Sport, and was the founding Chair of the British Philosophy of Sport Association.

Verner Møller is Professor, and head of the research unit 'Sport and Body Culture' at the Department of Sport Science, University of Aarhus, Denmark. He has written and edited books on extreme sports, doping, health and obesity. His research interest is mainly focused on problems of elite sport and body cultural extremes. His most recent books published in English are: *The Essence of Sport* (University of Southern Denmark Press, 2003) edited in collaboration with John Nauright, and *Doping and Public Policy* (University of Southern Denmark Press, 2004), edited in collaboration with John Hoberman. Currently he is writing a book, *Sport and Drugs*, which will be published by Berg Publishers in spring 2007, and his newest book in Danish is *Det Gyldne Fedt* (*The Golden Fat*) Gyldendal, 2006.

Robert E. Rinehart is Adjunct Professor in the Department of Kinesiology at California State University, San Bernadino. He is the author of *Players All: Performances in Contemporary Sport* (Indiana University Press) and co-editor of *To the Extreme: Alternative Sports, Inside and Out* (SUNY Press). His major research focus is in examining alternative sports forms, particular those considered 'extreme' and on the cusp between popular culture and mainstream sports.

Simon Robertson completed his PhD in philosophy at the University of St Andrews, Scotland, in 2005 and is currently a temporary lecturer at the University of Leeds, England. His main philosophical research lies at the inter-section of metaethics, practical reason and normative ethics. Outside philosophy, Simon's abiding interests are in various mountain pursuits.

Acknowledgements

It is my pleasure to thank the contributors of this volume for their original essays. I hope that they variously bring philosophy to bear on the kinds of activities that are often not thought of as belonging to the family of sports activities. In illuminating a wide array of philosophical problems in adventure sports, they also reveal the value of philosophical thought applied to these activities. In this regard, I hope they will stimulate readers who might not otherwise have been drawn to philosophical discussions of sports and also stimulate philosophers of sport to think beyond the dominant conceptions of sports in their own teaching and research.

Additionally, I would like to record my thanks to Andrew Bloodworth for his proofreading and corrections, Samantha Grant from Routledge for persuading me of the value of this project, and to Simon Eassom whose original idea the volume was.

1 Adventurous activity, prudent planners and risk

Mike McNamee

Introduction

That there are people in the world who are interested in risk and risk-taking would surprise no-one I venture. That there should be such a thing as the philosophy of sport, and a well-established tradition of scholarship in it, surprises most academics I meet.[1] That there might be philosophers, professionally interested in adventure, risk and risk-taking may well, however, raise more than a few eyebrows. Some further words are in order then.

A person sceptical of the legitimacy of these interests might well ask: 'Aren't philosophers to be found in their dust-crusted studies; wearing slippers and ancient woollen sweaters pondering the meaning of great theses?' Or, less ironically: 'What do they know of wild water, falling from the sky, climbing mountains and traversing ice and snow with ski or board, who pride themselves merely on clarifying the nature of thought and language and their relations to the world?' Or, perhaps the more informed and comically inclined might ask: 'Is it not the case that the only slippery slopes they know of are the ones from informal logic?' Such a set of biases is not entirely unfounded given the stereotypes of philosophy and philosophers. The aim of this volume, in some small way, is to put such preconceptions to rest. Yet there is more than mere caprice or ignorance at the heart of these preconceptions. Is there not something in the idea that rational reflection leads us away from risk and the kinds of activities called 'adventure sports?' To my mind there is. And it is to be found, at least partly, in the elision of the concepts of prudence and rationality both in everyday thinking and in philosophy. It is this relation – between 'prudence' and 'rationality' – that will be the object of these introductory remarks about the idea of a philosophical interest in adventure sports and risk. By way of introducing the present volume, I want to formulate some brief philosophical thoughts about one's commitment to the ways of life espoused here, and in so doing make manifest the kind of contribution philosophical activity can make to the theory and practice of adventure sports.

Rawls's rational planner and its progeny

One powerful statement of the rational requirements of prudence in the living of a good life, and the ordering of a just society, is to be found in the writings of John Rawls in his magnum opus *A Theory of Justice* (1971), which is widely credited with resurrecting normative political philosophy in the West at least. And in the subsequent writings of Norman Daniels's *Am I my Parent's Keeper?* (1988) in the philosophy of healthcare and on down into the philosophy of sport itself in the shape of Miller Brown's 1990 presidential address to the International Association for the Philosophy of Sport, *Practices and Prudence*, this fruitful line of though has been ploughed.

Rawls argues that it is definitive of our very idea of personhood that it should entail the capacity to formulate a rational plan of life. Persons are thus rational animals with the capacity to formulate a life plan. One of the great problems of modernity is that these life plans are not merely heterogeneous but conflicting. Thus the state is left, rather like a referee or umpire in a game, to mediate between the competing accounts while treating all parties in a just manner. One further and significant problem is how precisely one is to develop the rules of procedure to fairly enable ways of life that do not unfairly impinge on others. Rawls invokes a now famous thought experiment: 'the veil of ignorance'. Imagine, he says, that all rational agents must choose the rules for the governance of peoples from behind a veil that occludes all their identifying characteristics. Denied access to their situatedness, their age, culture, ethnicity, gender, spiritual beliefs, talents and so on the may come fairly and rationally to rules that can be used to order the just society. Unaware of their contingent characteristics the planner opts for prudence setting minimal rules that privilege no-one *ab initio*.

This idea is developed significantly in Daniel's 'prudential lifespan account' and introduces the metaphysical work of Derek Parfit (1984) on personhood and rationality. Daniels argues that the rational person will employ prudence in making decisions with regards to their life in time-neutral ways; avoiding the over-weighting of any given time slice. In the sports domain the 'prudential athletic lifestyle (PAL)' (Brown, 1990: 78) demands that a rational agent will engage in sport with a concern for their well-being over an entire life, ensuring that the goods inherent in sport can be pursued and secured over the course of a lifetime. Brown argues that prudence requires an individual to be '*equally* concerned about *all* the parts of his [sic] future' (ibid.: 78) thus keeping our options open.

Imagine, though, a biographical dimension here in order to explore the idea of this rational planning. It is not unlikely that many readers of this book, most of the contributing authors, and absolutely certainly the editor, are past their sporting prime. Our relative highpoints are behind us. For some of us, and here I speak for myself, they weren't very high but they are very much behind. So when we talk with the vibrant youth of our chosen athletic and adventurous pursuits, we might well hark back to particular first ascents, or to heavy training schedules, dreadful injuries, personal bests, peaks of skill and strategic thinking under conditions of compressed time and uncertain outcomes, and so on. In these remembrances we make our connections with the threads of sporting lives, past and present, and future too. By contrast, the rational planner of Brown's argument is the sportsperson who has no need for regret or self-reproach; s/he has enjoyed the goods of sport in childhood, youth, prime, middle age and maturity as a consequent of a rationally planned lifetime of prudent sporting. It's not so much prudent fiscal planning for old age, but prudent physical planning for the enjoyment of a lifetime of activity. What could be saner and more sensible? Brown's view goes to the heart of questions regarding our athletic careers and identities; it suffuses the question we ought ask ourselves most generally: how ought we to plan for and engage in sports over the course of a lifetime with equal regard to the whole of that lifetime?

Brown's prudent athletic planner: a critique

To what extent are activities we engage in now both of present value and future value? Put another way: to what extent are they properly thought to be also a preparation for later ages, and in particular old age? Is it not possible to argue that certain periods of life have more significance for the evaluation of one's living a good life? Is it necessarily true that all life periods are of equal importance? Arguing to the contrary, Slote writes that:

> Someone who understands the character of his own life must have some sort of view of its different periods, but must also be aware of its finitude. But this fact of finitude has important repercussions for our attitudes towards the different epochs of a single life. Older people sometimes envy the young for having so much of their lives left to live, and the young, in turn, often feel sorry for older people because they have so little time remaining. Having a substantial amount of time left is thus often thought to be of positive value, and judgments about how fortunate a given person is at a given time seem to depend not only on what is happening to him and what he is doing at that time, but on our estimation of how much time the person can reasonably count on in the future.
>
> (Slote, 1983: 34)

A corollary of this view might be that we should consider the unity of life to be understood in the context of finitude. Might this not give us reason to value certain lifetime slices more than others without being drawn to the idea that we are necessarily irrational? Why is temporal egalitarianism thought to be obligatory for the prudent-rational planner? It is not for no reason that the utilitarians thought propinquity and certainty were criteria for moral judgements. Other things being equal we ought to prefer those acts whose satisfactions are nearer in time or more certain to be the consequences of our actions. Of course the key idea here is 'other things being equal'. And how are we fully to know the conditions of the future in our planning rationally for it? I think that these ideas can be related to some very common intuitions regarding the arc of a human life. It is not only biologists who are committed to the view of this arc of human existence between inception, development and decay. Economists, following a common-sensical approach, note that our bio-psychological powers experience decay and deleterious effects as we age. This is the brute fact of senescence. What implications do these facts have for rational planners as risk-seekers and adventure enthusiasts? Well, at least this: that these initially increasing and later diminishing abilities themselves influence our capacity to experience enjoyment and satisfaction therein (Trostel and Taylor, 2004). Do not many of us – with heydays gone – consider ourselves beyond a peak, a notion of maturity, of life's being lived to the fullest of life's leading 'up to' . . . or 'down from' a high point (Slote, 1983)? Why save so much for later periods of life the like of which we may not be able to enjoy? Now while Brown does not say it, the reader is left with the very strong impression that rationally one must regard well-being as time-neutral and that we must be prudent in our planning in order to respect this metaphysical aspect of personhood: rational persons simply must be prudent persons. He writes:

> At any one time when we are young we are inclined to pursue our current projects to the fullest ability and resources. But a prudential outlook requires us to keep in mind that at later stages of our lives we may well have different projects, different allegiances, and different priorities and values, and we will then also need to call on our abilities and resources to satisfy the demands of these stages. In our prudential reflections we must be able to abstract from our present concerns and allow for later passions. We cannot, prudentially, commit all now with no thought to what prospects and projects we may then face, ones *likely to be quite different* from those that entice and fulfil us now and yet every bit as alluring.
>
> (Brown, 1990: 78, emphasis added)

At this point Brown moves on from Parfit and Daniels to Rawls to find the technique that will deliver the kind of abstraction from the present and the particular that corrupts our prudence. Thus Brown invokes Rawls's veil of ignorance noted in outline above. Prudent athletic persons with no knowledge of their particularity are epistemically restricted 'to avoid age bias' (ibid.: 79). They therefore choose rationally and prudently, not knowing whether they will benefit from given future events. These three elements form Brown's Prudential Athletic Lifestyle:

> A prudential viewpoint is inherently a cautious one, one that forgoes extremes with an eye to later enjoyments. In our goal to keep our options open and not to discount the importance of any stages of our lives, we expend our resources warily: Profligacy is prohibited.
>
> (ibid.)

And profligacy, he asserts, is the problem of youth: 'The problem is most clear in the contrast between youth and age, the former inclined to risk all, the latter to spend little' (ibid.). Now in this regard Brown follows a well-trodden path, one travelled by philosophers and social commentators alike. Remember George Bernard Shaw's quip: 'Youth is a wonderful thing. What a crime to waste it on children.' In attempting to give perspective to the follies of youth, parents and pedagogues (such as myself) tend to warn those whose life plans are unformed and uninformed of the dangers of committing all and all too hastily in this or that endeavour. Brown, then, is not alone in his general sentiment that 'chronological parochialism' (ibid.) is to be avoided.

What this entails for Brown, however, is either the foregoing of sports participation that entails unreasonable risks or – where the significant risks are inherent within the sport – the elimination of those sports entirely. In relation to Rawls's philosophical anthropology, Barber (1975) summarises what is equally applicable to Brown:

> Rawlsian man in the original position is finally a striking lugubrious creature: unwilling to enter a situation that promises success because it also promises failure, unwilling to risk winning because he feels doomed to losing, ready for the worst because he cannot imagine the best, content with the security and the knowledge he will be no worse off than anyone else because he dares to risk freedom and the possibility that he will be better off under all guises of 'rationality'.
>
> (Barber, 1975: 299)

Beyond the timid philosophical anthropology at the heart of the veil of ignorance thought experiment, there is a further consequence of adopting a Rawlsian approach for Brown's thesis, the unpopularity of which he recognises. Athletes considering engaging in adventurous and risk-laden pursuits must either forego participation when it entails unreasonable risks or where the significant risks are inherent within the sport, they should acquiesce to the elimination of those sports entirely. Nevertheless, in demanding that we keep our options Brown assumes that our future projects are 'likely to be quite different' – but how can he know this in advance? Moreover, his position also rather begs the question as to what is going to count as a relevant time slice. And he nowhere comments on these matters. So, compare my relatively settled dispositions, attachments, and projects now, in my mid-forties, with those that will adhere in my sixties. Why are they 'likely' to be different? At what level? How much open-endedness do I need to plan for? What kind of old age shall I live to? So it seems we can prudently count the future in, without giving it equal weight. And even if we were to do so, what latitude does keeping our options open require and for how long? In short, what is the economy of prudent planning? Is Brown's prudent planner the right kind of model for personal planning?

The rational life plan and the prudent self

If we object, then, to the manoeuvre of the veil of ignorance for the reasons above, and of course there might be many other criticisms (such as the asocial individualism it embodies), we might allow persons to have relevant knowledge of their particularities, prospects and projects. Perhaps this will enable them to plan prudently for a lifetime of athletic activity thereby observing the principle of time-neutrality of well-being without necessarily being committed to an anthropology that is as risk-aversive as Brown's prudent planner. Rawls's use of the idea of a life plan,[2] however, which is adopted by Brown, leads one to question the nature and scope of the rationality that underwrites the very idea of a plan of life. Indeed the idea of a life plan, though it might find a home in other social scientific thinking, seems a particularly philosophical predilection.

Larmore writes that:

> The canonical view among philosophers ancient and modern has been, in essence, that the life lived well is the life lived in accord with a rational plan. To me this conception of the human good seems manifestly wrong. The idea that life should be the object of a plan is false to the human condition. It misses the important truth which Proust, by contrast, discerned and made into one of the organizing themes of his great meditation on disappointment and revelation, *A la recherche du temps perdu*: The happiness that life affords is less often the good we have reason to pursue than the good that befalls us unexpectedly.
>
> (Larmore, 1999: 99)

The received picture is one where persons do not allow themselves so much to be at the mercy of the slings and arrows of outrageous fortune. The distinction is neatly captured in the idea that we should lead our own lives rather than be led by them, merely allowing things to move us. The underlying distinction of course is the activity characteristic of a human agent rather than its passivity. Nussbaum (2001), locating tragedy in the ancient myths, has fruitfully explored the feature of good lives that are also beset by tragedy; a paradigm of passivity one might think. One central message in Nussbaum's *Fragility of Goodness* is that we cannot inure ourselves to luck. Now this in itself is not a blinding insight, a sceptic might think. But two points have to be made to understand it properly. First, it is not that we simply cannot fully see the future in order to plan rationally for it. More than this, secondly, we have to be open to the different possibilities that life may put our way. And this is precisely a corollary of the view held by many adventure enthusiasts that modern life is timid, cautious, run on socially (pre)determined and economically cautious lines.[3] Imagine how this process happens in 'limit cases' such as religious conversions; or significantly adapting one's lifestyle after a heart attack; of course, a career-ending injury; or coming to terms with a new sense of a disabled self after disease or a car crash.

To this point Larmore adds two others: our conceptions of the good are limited by our experiences to date and this necessarily – to some degree or another – falls short of what life yet has in store for us. If we fail to appreciate surprise by a hitherto unplanned-for good, we take away one feature of life that makes it worth living.

One root of Rawls's rationalism is that although the unreflective life is not worth living, we tend to view it from the perspective of an unbiased agent, a third person, or indeed a time-less, space-less perspective (the view from nowhere). Now Williams (1985) has offered a critique of this perspective: there is no Archimedean point from which to plan the good life. Larmore's objection is the result of the would-be viewpoint: what we reason towards. A variation of this point serves as the introduction of Richard Wollheim's book *The Thread of Life*: where do we reason from? He draws from Kirkegaard's journal for 1843 which opens:

> It is perfectly true, as philosophers say, that life must be understood backwards. But they forget the other proposition, that it must be lived forwards. And if one thinks over that proposition it becomes more and more evident that life can never really be understood in time simply because at no particular moment can I find the necessary resting-place from which to understand it backwards.
>
> (Wollheim, 1984: 1)

Wollheim's claim is that a life is a product, but the living of a life is a process and needs to be understood processually.

By contrast, Rawls's picture, utilised by Brown, is one where we can live a prudent life by executing a life plan from nowhere in particular within the world and knowing only that we have to keep our options open. This looks rather like being able to have one's cake and eat it. But the good life is not the same as the prudent life – this much Brown acknowledges.

It strikes me that what is required here is a more anthropocentric practical reason than is on offer in Rawls's veil of ignorance and the rational deliberations of his life plan and prudent life planner which Brown expropriates. That picture of practical reason must be one which is attuned to our nature and our ethical sensibilities which includes but supercedes vegetative and animal existence. And we can find a better picture of this rational-moral drive within the anthropocentric view of Aristotle who, as Ackrill puts it:

> certainly does think that the nature of man – the powers and needs all men have – determines the character that any satisfying human life must have. But since his account of the nature of man is in general terms the corresponding specification of the best life for man is also general. So while his assumption puts some limits on the possible answers to the question 'how shall I live?' it leaves considerable scope for a discussion which takes account of my individual tastes, capacities, and circumstances.
>
> (Ackrill, 1973: 13)

Moving (adventurously) on

What the contributors of this volume offer are rich and varied accounts of the way in which inherently risky activities are pursued for the joys and satisfactions they bring to a life, but not in an irrational or carefree way. Adventurous risk-takers are commonly prudent about their planning; they check and double check equipment, terrain, timings and weather forecasts. Moreover, they realise that prudent planning and luck, far from incompatible with risk taking, are part and parcel of it when properly conceived. Thus adventurous sportspersons project into the future to understand the shape of their lives, both prudent and good, but certainly not in time-neutral ways. Considering the ways they do this, reflecting philosophically on the nature and goals of their pursuits and their own informed desires and identities, is the process of coming to know what kind of athletic engagement should figure in their lives. It is of course true that in many, and perhaps most, cases we are wise to avoid *radical* time-preference. Yet this does not entail a time-neutralising attitude to our well-being. We must acknowledge, nevertheless, that there are those for whom *considered* risk-taking, the *joie de vivre* to be found in the imminence of adventure, the élan of gliding on the pistes, the climbing of challenging crags, or in free bird-like falling, or reading and riding wild water, is the very essence of the good life.

Notes

1 But such there is. The International Association for the Philosophy of Sport was established in the United States of America in 1972 under the leadership of the celebrated Catholic philosopher, Paul Weiss under the name 'Philosophic Society for the Study of Sport'. Its journal, *Journal of the Philosophy of Sport*, has been publishing high-quality philosophical papers ever since and has recently been joined by another journal in the field *Sport, Ethics and Philosophy*, which is some testament to the renewed interest in philosophical and particularly ethical aspects of sport.
2 It is not merely Rawls that has employed this idea. Among contemporary philosophers Charles Taylor (1985) has made important use of it, although his account of person-hood is much less rationalistic. I have elsewhere given account of the possibilities of Taylor's account which is much more sympathetic to the emotions, and its signifi-cance for sporting activities in McNamee (1992). Yet the idea goes back further to the writings of Josiah Royce at the turn of the twentieth century. See Larmore (1999: 102–3).
3 As I come to think of it: the kind of life I lead.

References

Ackrill, J. (1973) *Aristotle: Ethics*, London: Faber.
Barber, B. R. (1975) 'Justifying Justice: Problems of Psychology, Politics and Measurement', in *Reading Rawls*, Oxford: Blackwell, 292–318.
Brown, W. M. (1990) 'Practices and Prudence', *Journal of the Philosophy of Sport*, XVII: 71–84.
Daniels, N. (1998) *Am I my Parent's Keeper?*, New York: Oxford University Press.
Larmore, C. (1999) 'The Idea of a Life Plan', in E. F. Paul, F. D. Miller and J. Paul (eds) *Human Flourishing*, Cambridge: Cambridge University Press.

McNamee, M. J. (1992) 'Physical Education and the Development of Personhood', *Physical Education Review*, 15 (1): 13–28.

Nussbaum, M. C. (2001) *The Fragility of Goodness*, Cambridge: Cambridge University Press.

Parfit, D. (1984) *Reasons and Persons*, Oxford: Oxford University Press.

Slote, M. (1983) *Goods and Virtues*, Oxford: Clarendon Press.

Taylor, C. (1985) *Philosophical Papers 1: Human Agency and Language*, Cambridge: Cambridge University Press.

Trostel, P. A. and Taylor, G. A. (2004) 'A Theory of Time Preference', *Economic Inquiry*, 39 (3): 379–95.

Williams, B. A. O. (1985) *Ethics and the Limits of Philosophy*, London: Fontana/Collins.

Wollheim, R. (1984) *The Thread of Life*, Cambridge: Cambridge University Press.

2 The quest for excitement and the safe society

Gunnar Breivik

Introduction

In 1926, two years before he died, Fridtjof Nansen, the Norwegian Arctic explorer, scientist and humanist, gave a speech at St Andrews University in Scotland. The speech had the title 'Adventure' and Nansen talked about the human need for challenges:

> It is our perpetual yearning to overcome difficulties and dangers, to see the hidden things, to penetrate into the regions outside our beaten track – it is the call of the unknown – the longing for the land of Beyond, the driving force deeply rooted in the soul of man which drove the first hunters into new regions – the mainspring perhaps of our greatest actions – of winged human thought knowing no bounds to its freedom
>
> (Nansen, 1927: 20)

He did, however, speak not only about the deep longing for the ultimate challenges, but also about our everyday lives, 'You have to take risks, and cannot allow yourself to be frightened by them when you are convinced that you are following the right course. Nothing worth having in life is ever attained without taking risks' (ibid.: 36). Now one could think that these are the words of a very special person; a risk-taking explorer. What might ordinary citizens say on the matter?

In a national survey (Norsk Monitor, 2003) of opinions, attitudes, values and behaviour in a representative sample of the Norwegian population above 15 years, 10 per cent agreed completely and 37 per cent to some extent to the statement 'I am willing to take big chances to get what I want out of life' (ibid.: 29). That means that around half of the population is to some extent willing to take big chances in life. When one bears in mind that this includes not only the young and daring men, but the total population above 15 years, it is a strong indicator of a need for taking chances that is in total contrast to the idea of a safe society. Obviously there is a tension between, on one hand, the quest for excitement and thrills that according to Nansen is deeply rooted in human nature, and, on the other hand, the idea of a safe society that has been so central in modern welfare policies.

In light of these remarks, my aim in this chapter is threefold. First, I develop a realistic picture of human nature where also the thrills, excitements and risks have their place. Second, I enquire as to how this picture of 'humankind' is a realistic background for work on safety and control in all sectors of society. Finally, I show how this picture is a necessary background for the development of a thrill sector in modern society, especially related to sport, leisure, education and tourism. I will do this by drawing on knowledge from several scientific disciplines and knowledge areas.

Concepts and basic assumptions

Let us first take a look at some of the concepts that we use. We have concepts that refer to the general interest or need for thrills and excitement. Expressions like 'quest for excitement', 'thrill seeking', 'adventure seeking', 'need for stimulation' point to a general need for arousal, stimulation or novelty, and more specifically to a need for strong positive sensations or feelings, where ecstatic joy is the most extreme form. In psychological theories concepts like 'novelty seeking' are used to express this general disposition. A more specific trait, which has received a lot of attention, is called 'sensation seeking', which may be defined as 'the seeking of varied, novel, complex and intense sensations and experiences, and the willingness to take physical, social, legal, and financial risks for the sake of such experience' (Zuckerman, 1994: 27).

The quest for excitement, or more specifically sensation seeking, may involve but does not necessitate risk taking. Sometimes it seems as if risk taking in and of itself is a strong stimulation, and not only a consequence of, or an adjunct to, the seeking of strong sensations. 'Risk' is a concept that is used in several scientific and non-scientific contexts and with varying content. The concept first appeared in the Middle Ages, relating to maritime insurance (Lupton, 1999). In most cases risk seems to involve a loss of some kind (Yates and Stone, 1992). The loss may be related to economic or material factors, to social and personal factors, or to physical and mental factors (Breivik, 1999a). According to a long tradition in philosophy it is also possible to speak of existential risk that puts one's total life project in danger (Tillich, 1952).

In many theories in different scientific disciplines there is a concern for safety and control that becomes evident in the basic concepts. As Mary Douglas has repeatedly pointed out, these concepts and constructs have strong social and cultural underpinnings, and are not neutral or objective in any sense (Douglas and Wildavsky, 1982; Douglas, 1992). Embedded in the construction and use of these concepts are several basic assumptions about what constitutes 'normal' or 'acceptable behaviour'. Humans are, for instance, often supposed to be 'risk avoiding' and 'safety seeking'. 'Risk taking' is accepted as rational only under certain circumstances. In the discussion of the risk construct Yates and Stone point to the fact that several authors have stated that 'in isolation there is no such thing as acceptable risk; because by its very nature, risk should always be rejected' (Yates and Stone, 1992: 3). Other authors, like Adams (1995), think that people are not in general risk-aversive: 'Zero-risk man is a figment of the imagination of the safety profession. *Homo prudens* is but one aspect of the human character. *Homo aleatorius* – dice man, gambling man, risk-taking man – also lurks within every one of us' (Adams, 1995: 16).

To identify the cultural and normative underpinnings, it may be a good idea to make explicit the alternative levels of risk tolerance such as risk avoidance, risk acceptance, risk taking, or risk seeking. These levels refer to varying situational and personal constraints and possibilities. In some situations we must face risks that are imposed upon us. In other situations we can choose freely which level of risk we want, as when we are skiing in the mountains. In some situations we are aware of taking risks, in others not. There are a lot of other variations around the risk taking situation. Risk taking is not a natural but a many-layered construction.

To exemplify the differences in basic assumptions let me sketch two quite different basic normative attitudes to risk that may influence not only the choice of theories and hypotheses, but also the basic concepts. One basic normative attitude could be called 'Risk Aversion'. It would imply a belief that human beings are basically risk avoiding and safety seeking. They should therefore logically avoid risks whenever it is possible. One should always try to scan, detect, identify and control risks. When it is impossible to avoid risks, then one should choose the smallest. One should always avoid taking risks that involve other persons without their explicit consent. This would exemplify a normative risk aversive strategy.

An opposite basic normative attitude could be called 'Risk Acceptance'. It would imply that human beings should accept risks and even take risks under certain circumstances. One should, however, always try to identify and control risks. One should avoid or eliminate risks when there are no rewards. Risks should be minimized when other people are involved. One should, however, be willing to take risks when the rewards are obvious and the total expected outcome is positive. One should not only accept, but even seek, risks when the odds are good enough, mastery is possible and the total expected outcome is positive.

In my view we find in modern societies an increasing support of the risk aversion attitude. Risks should be eliminated or at least avoided and minimized. In this chapter I argue that there are many good reasons to give support to a more risk accepting attitude. This does not mean that we should not try to make people more rational in their dealing with risk. On the other hand we should be careful to transfer scientific ideals of risk and uncertainty to ordinary life. It may not be a good idea to make people into risk processing machines or to give an illusion of too exact information about the future. As Bernstein says about the economist Keynes, 'Rather than frightening us, Keynes' words bring great news: we are not prisoners of an inevitable future. Uncertainty makes us free' (Bernstein, 1996: 229). Uncertainty may be better than probability. 'Where everything works according to the laws of probability, we are like primitive people – or gamblers – who have no recourse but to recite incantations to their gods' (ibid.: 229). Also

Adams thinks that uncertainty is important: 'We respond to the promptings of *Homo aleatorius* because we have no choice: life is uncertain. And we respond because we want to: Too much certainty is boring, unrewarding and belittling' (Adams, 1995: 17). Like Keynes he thinks uncertainty makes us what we are: 'Only if there is uncertainty is there scope for responsibility and conscience. Without it we are mere predetermined automata' (ibid.: 18). This means, according to Keynes and Adams, that we are free, our decisions matter, we can change the world. In order to master the world we should not rely upon our probability calculus but upon our skills and mastery. We should confront danger and take calculated risks, but only when we have developed the necessary skills and experiential tools.

Two social cosmologies: risk versus safety

We find historical paradigms and examples of both risk acceptance and risk avoidance. Some social cosmologies favour attitudes where members of the society enter risky arenas and confront dangers by using their skills to the uttermost limit. However, we also find societies that encourage their members to control risks and base their lives on safety mechanisms, whether real or hypothetical. I think the original paradigms for these differing social cosmologies go back at least to the beginning of Western philosophy. Two thousand, five hundred years ago two Greek philosophers gave us two quite opposite views of the world, of *kosmos*. Heraclitus from Ephesus (500 BC) thought of cosmos as a dynamic process where everything was moving, changing. For Heraclitus the essence of cosmos is captured in metaphors like the streaming water in a river, the licking flames of a fire, the opposite sides of a *polemos*, a fight, the dynamic tension between the bow and string which makes the arrow fly. The world is a world of opposites, of light and dark, up and down, sweet and sour, pleasure and pain. This dynamic tension between opposites is the *dynamis*, the power of change. The deep nature of cosmos is that *panta rei*, everything flows or runs.

Parmenides from Elea (500 BC) thought that the cosmos was a huge round ball, which was in complete rest. Change and movement are illusions: 'Trust your thinking and not your senses.' Thinking tells us that the world is perfect and therefore it has to have the perfect shape of roundness and it has to be still. Parmenides' student Zeno tried in several examples to show how we end up with paradoxes when we accept that motion is possible, for instance in the famous story of Heracles who was unable to overtake the turtle.

The thought forms of Heraclitus and Parmenides shaped our Western tradition. We find the tension between the two views in many contexts as a tension between movement and rest, process and structure, the dynamic and the static, growth and stability, risk and safety. The paradigmatic views of the two Greek philosophers are to differing degrees realized in historical societies. There is an interesting study by the climber and anthropologist Mike Thompson (1980) which shows how different environments and ways of living shape different risk strategies in two different cultures. The Hindu culture of sedentary cattle farmers south of the Himalayas is quite different from the sheep herding nomads on the north side of the Himalayas. The Hindus are safety seeking and try to spread both risks and rewards. One should help one's neighbour and one should expect help in return. The Buddhists are risk takers who concentrate both risk and rewards. It is typically the Buddhists that have raised and equipped caravans over the high mountain passes in order to trade from south to north and from north to south. One needs to take economical, physical and social risks to do this and one may become very rich or very poor. Interestingly enough Thompson found that the Hindus were in many ways pessimistic in their outlook and the Buddhists were optimists. In many ways the Buddhists seem to represent the Heraclitan world-view. The world is a changing, uncertain place where one has to master risks in order to stay alive. One has to be alert. The Hindus seem to have more of a Parmenidean world-view, which includes the wish for stability and predictability, but with a pessimistic undertone since the world after all is unstable.

Differing social cosmologies are attached to different cultures and societies. But we can also find differing and even conflicting cosmologies running as opposing strains through one and the same society. Norway has on one hand a 'coast culture' based on fishing, shipping, trade and the oil industry. This culture in many ways expresses a risk accepting attitude. On the other hand we have an 'inland culture' based on farming and industry that express a more risk aversive attitude. Church and state support and underscore risk aversion and seek to develop safety and security as fundamental values. In a survey of peoples' attitudes we actually find that the coastal people are more willing to take risks (Norsk Monitor, 2003). One reason for this is probably the long adaptation to a shifting and insecure environment that favours the open and risk accepting attitude. In his celebrated novel about the nineteenth-century fishermen who sailed to Lofoten in northern Norway for cod fishery, Johan Bojer (2005) told how these fishermen not only accepted the necessary risk. They challenged the wind and the waves, took risks and loved the competition between the boats.

We can even go further. Maybe risk and safety are complementary factors, not only in world-views, between cultures, inside a culture, between individuals (as we shall see later), but also inside individuals or persons. Moxnes (1989) has developed a psychological theory, where not only the need for safety and security is stressed, but also the need for growth, challenges and risks. Each person needs a basic safety, an ontological security, which they should get during the first years of life. On the other hand we undergo a fabulous development from conception, through birth, when growing up and until we die. It is impossible to grow and develop under full security. Therefore we need to accept chances and risks. This factor is, according to Moxnes, closely tied to our need for freedom. On the other hand our need for security is tied to our search for meaning and roots. Our life should, according to this view, make a spiral from one level of security, through risky leaps and stages of growth, to higher levels of stability. This means that there should be a place in people's individual lives as well as in societies for challenges and risks. The modern societies have tended to put too much emphasis on security. Let us look closer at why this is so and what it implies.

The modern idea of the rational safety seeker

In many ways modern industrial society is obsessed with safety and control. We are not only obsessed with control but we have also developed a culture of fear. Frank Furedi (1997) points to the increasing risk consciousness in modern societies. People are afraid of hidden dangers everywhere. This is in sharp contrast to the fact 'that despite the many problems that face humanity, we live in a world that is far safer than at any time in history' (Furedi, 1997: 54). Furedi thinks that 'The exaggeration of problems and risks is only matched by the denigration of the problem-solving potential of people. On the basis of such a negative representation of people, it is difficult to motivate or inspire society' (ibid.: 164).

Even if the problem solving capacity of people is denigrated and undermined the solution of the problem for many still seems to lie in the direction of rational control. According to Lupton:

> the emphasis in contemporary western societies on the avoidance of risk is strongly associated with the ideal of the 'civilized' body, an increasing desire to take control over one's life, to rationalize and regulate the self and the body, to avoid the vicissitudes of fate. To take unnecessary risks is commonly seen as foolhardy, careless, irresponsible, and even 'deviant', evidence of an individual's ignorance or lack of ability to regulate the self.
>
> (Lupton, 1999: 148)

The need for control is even more salient in society at large. Modern society has become a huge industrial, technological and economic monster structure that simply must not collapse. One doesn't play with an atomic reactor. Therefore modern society can only survive if it succeeds in taming humans into rational, safety seeking creatures. Such a view of human beings emerged during the Enlightenment period in the eighteenth century. The idea of modernism encompassed progress, science, rationality and control as central factors (Harvey, 1991). The goal was to create a 'dominion of man' that could control nature and bring happiness to all human beings. The new industrial and technological society that was developed in the nineteenth and the twentieth century, presupposed the docile and tamed 'animal rationale'. Without control over impulses and needs and a rational, long-term perspective on one's own behaviour and thinking, it is impossible to run a complex, fragile technological society in a safe way. The many failures and problems in introducing modern technology and lifestyle in so-called Third World cultures are, according to many experts, due to the lack of the modernistic ethos in these cultures. They often lack the long-term planning, the achievement motivation, the control of needs and impulses, the sense of well-tempered pleasure and the concern for safety that has become endemic in the industrialized world. But this attitude, even in Western societies, is only skin deep; it is not deeply rooted in human nature. The many accidents and problems show that irrationality lurks under the surface of rationality. It seems that we have a 'beast within', that sometimes and under certain circumstances, makes us thrill seekers who not only accept risk but even seek it.

A lack of fit between modern society and human nature?

I am not in line with behaviourism and other psychological or anthropological views, according to which we humans are entirely malleable. We are not born as a 'tabula rasa', a blank tablet. Some people seem to think that it would have been nice if we had been malleable, and could be formed, developed, shaped and adapted to natural and cultural environments. For work on safety such malleability would have been nice, since we could have developed the necessary relation of fit between humankind and modern society and thereby improved safety and security.

It becomes increasingly evident, however, that human nature and modern society do not fit with each other as a hand into a glove, or as a key into a lock. There are mismatches between human nature and modern society that is evident in many sectors and particularly (for our purposes) in relation to safety. One can see the problems both from the side of the individual human being and from the side of society. The risks that are not handled well may have several causes. Some of them are outside our control. Accidents happen due to chance, bad luck, complexity, time factors and so on. Others happen because of human factors. Accidents are caused by fatigue, lack of concentration, lack of attention and foresight. Some are due to strong emotions, irrationality, bad temper, irritability, aggressiveness or stress. And at other times people simply lack the skills, do not understand things, or lack the necessary insight. As the studies of heuristics in risk taking have shown, people have many illusions concerning objective security and risk (Kahneman *et al.*, 1986). A special case is, however, the type of situations where we simply are not concerned about safety, as the only motive and want to take risks in a conscious and calculated way. Should we handle this motive as something that should be suppressed, sublimated or avoided, since it is contrary to a safety seeking attitude, or should we accept this 'beast within' as part of human nature and try to handle it in the best possible way. There are strong reasons why I think we should accept the 'beast within'. One of the reasons I think lies in our evolutionary heritage.

Evolutionary anthropology shows how humans were adapted to, and formed by, shifting environments through the last millions of years from *Homo habilis*, or earlier, to the present human being (Staski and Marks, 1992; Buss, 1988). The general picture given by these evolutionary approaches is very different from the picture of humans that in varying shapes have been presented in the last 200–300 years by the bourgeois culture in Europe. The bourgeois picture projected the human being as a frail and weak creature that had to compensate the lack of bodily strength through a well-developed brain and the use of symbolic powers like language, communication and abstract thinking. The evolutionary picture portrays humans as beings with considerable bodily strength and robustness. Humans developed as hunter-gatherers through 2 million years of evolution, from

question the timing of the reflection, not the claim that OKEs offer opportunity for insight. Tales told in camp or at home, and the many books, essays, films, and conferences on OKEs are forms of reflection that helps us not only to recall the events, but also to see implications, clarify connections to other ideas, and bring out the significant ideas from our outdoor experiences. Such reflection helps us to regain balance, to understand nature's force, to compare movement in varied contexts, to place things in order, and to marvel at the beauty around us.

OKEs involve us in energetic responses to locations in nature that show evidence of minimal human management. When we move swiftly through nature we inject our own energy into the activity and in so doing develop a sense of ownership for the experience that we can achieve in no other way. Such motion paradoxically releases energy through using it. It will be argued in the next two sections that such energetic interactions expand our ways of knowing, i.e. our epistemology, and offer us the opportunity for aesthetic experiences.

Epistemology in nature

OKEs can expand, enrich, and enliven our epistemology, but the relation between OKEs and epistemology requires explanation. Epistemology is the name given to the study of the nature and values of human knowledge. One part of epistemology concerns knowledge that guides deliberate action or conduct. When knowledge guides conduct, as is the case in OKEs, the excellence or perfection of such knowledge is 'phronesis' or practical wisdom. Josef Pieper discusses foresight that is a prerequisite for phronesis. Foresight is 'the capacity to estimate, with a sure instinct for the future, whether a particular action will lead to the realization of the goal' (Pieper, 1966: 18). Foresight occurs before an event and allows us to remain attentive to our goals. Pieper continues and presents the basic elements of the intellectual virtue of phronesis: verifiable memory, open-mindedness, and something he calls perfected ability, which is the capacity to act swiftly with clear-sighted vision in fast moving situations (ibid.: 17). An example of a verifiable memory relevant to OKEs is the memory of sailing skills that are verified as soon as the wind hits the sails. Open-mindedness will be discussed presently. Perfected ability closely resembles what will be referred to below as ecological rationality.

Moving in nature demands that we engage and develop the virtue of phronesis, which means we know what it is in the environment that we must to attend to and then act. OKEs involve a package deal. We must engage foresight in preparation and then, once engaged in the OKE, make our best estimates of a given situation with goals in mind. In addition we must engage our foresight and make our estimations with limited time and information. When we guide our choices with reference to such conditions, we practice phronesis. In the spirit of learning from mistakes, let me offer a personal example when phronesis was not practiced.

Those who sail twin-hulled catamarans know they must attend to many things when the goal is to move smoothly and safely. The crew's weight, for example, must balance so that both bows remain above the water as often as possible. In forceful wind when the boat tilts, the lower bow can come dangerously close to the water. One day my boat's lower bow caught a deep wave and we flipped stern over bow. Moments before the accident I had positioned myself forward toward the bows and was watching carefully as the lower bow went ever deeper into the waves, yet my foresight, my sure instinct for the future, failed to function. I saw the danger but did not act accordingly, even though I had time to act. A more knowledgeable sailor than I, one practiced in the practical wisdom of sailing, would have seen the predicament and instantly shifted weight to balance the boat. This is not to claim that the sailor could not have thought or spoken, only that the phronesis-guided action of a well-trained person could have been automatic, efficient, effective, and without any verbal intervention.

Open-mindedness, as it relates to OKEs, requires us to expand our knowledge repertoire with special attention to knowledge that comes to us through the body, so-called body wisdom, because OKEs place physical demands on us (Armstrong, 1993: 77). Our body can often detect a need in an OKE and react to it before we could place it in a language framework. As Michael Polanyi famously said, 'We know more than we can tell' (Polanyi, 1966: 4). For example, someone snorkeling may be inattentive to the tide that is slowly pulling them away from shore, but all the while their body wordlessly keeps alert to changing conditions, initiates swimming motions toward shore, and generally frees the swimmer's attention for other things.

When the wisdom of our body interacts with the physical reality of an OKE, it becomes a means to knowledge, and in the process we expand our epistemology. As my sailing tale suggests, success in learning, in opening ourselves to new knowledge, does not require a successful OKE. Failure can energize us to cultivate greater foresight, which we can then export to other experiences. The phronesis demanded by OKEs thus expands our epistemological stock.

OKEs help us with a form of learning that may have played a role in evolution, a form that Peter Todd calls ecological rationality. This form of gathering knowledge expands our epistemology to include the need to make decisions quickly, as is often the case in OKEs. Todd says in ecological rationality we detect, 'features of the external environment [that] would have strong adaptive pressures, particularly the need to minimize time by minimizing the search for information' (Todd, 2001: 51). Humans evolved by gathering information necessary to survive and flourish. Not all relevant information, however, could be considered because our cave-dwelling ancestors had to move swiftly to get the food before other creatures did: move fast or starve.

Ecological rationality involves sampling the environment and making educated guesses under conditions where time is limited and dangers are real. Ecological rationality represents an adaptive modification of rationality, not a new category of rationality. Todd argues that it is sound evolutionary thinking to say humans wisely use simple, quick, and time-efficient guides (i.e. heuristics) to help us sample in order to survive and flourish when facing threats. He writes, 'The human mind makes many decisions by drawing on an adaptive toolbox of simple heuristics . . . because these fast and information-frugal heuristics are well matched to the challenges of the . . . environment' (Todd, 2001: 52). When being chased by a saber-toothed tiger, for example, cave folks had to make quick decisions without the benefit of all possible information. Move fast or die.

OKEs also place time and information constraints on us. The weather changes during a rock climb: what do we do? Lightning sparks a fire on a backcountry hike: what do we do? A flash flood surprises us on the river: what do we do? Weather, fires, and floods are complex and could involve us in long hours of data gathering. However, the question 'What do we do?' tagged onto each scenario suggests an urgency that precludes full deliberation of all relevant information. Move fast or suffer.

OKEs expand epistemology in that they place demands on us that often arrive in unpredictable moments and require quick action on our part. OKEs give us practice with ecological rationality that allows us to 'exploit the representations and structures of information in the environment to make reasonable judgments and decisions' (Gigerenzer, 2000: 57). Notice the last comment entails the need to make reasonable judgments and decisions rather than perfect ones, or fully informed ones, or make them after complete deliberation. We sample, select, estimate, and make reasonable guesses because they generally work and they work in lives where decisions are forced on us with great haste. When we move on fast rivers and speed down steep paths, OKEs allow us to engage 'a cognitive system [that] is designed to find many pathways to the world, substituting missing cues with whatever cues happen to be available' (ibid.: 196). OKEs expand our repertoire of knowledge-gathering skills that we may have previously ignored because in familiar places we may have had time to conduct full inquiries and make robust decisions based on the best information. If our cognitive system is, as Gigerenzer claims, one designed to find multiple ways to know, where we must decide and act quickly and without all relevant information, then OKEs connect us with a neglected aspect of our thinking, our knowledge-gathering abilities, and finally our epistemology.

While we may overlook relevant evidence in ecological rationality, this does not mean it encourages self-deception. Self-deception involves willfully ignoring relevant evidence, not overlooking relevant evidence because a necessity for speed limits us. OKEs help us address self-deception.

Self-deception confounds epistemology because it ignores evidence and devalues honesty and candor. Self-deception allows us to select out those pieces of information that run counter to a favored outcome. The self-deceiver throws the dart into a blank wall and then paints a bulls-eye where it struck. Self-deceivers fool themselves into thinking one way when relevant information points in the other. An epistemology that includes self-deception is rife with inconsistencies, contradictions, vagaries, and incomplete information.

It may be the case that there cannot be full-blown, robust self-deception where an individual is both the deceiver and the deceived (Haight, 1980). Even accepting this conjecture, self-deception may still influence us because it may be partial and occasional rather than full-blown and robust. We may not do it all the time, only those times when weakness overcomes us. We are not thrown into a life of contradiction because, on occasion, we countenance a little self-deception. Though self-deceivers ignore evidence that contradicts a favored outcome, they have learned that in familiar places where they are in control, they can look the other way and often get away with it.

Looking the other way when, for example, we canoe a section of whitewater may prove difficult and dangerous because the motion and force of the water demands full attention. If we do not know what to do upon entering the rapids, if we engage in self-deception, then we will suffer.

Those who engage in OKEs should attend to as much relevant information as they can master, given the constraints of time and information. They should also know they must never intentionally ignore relevant information that dis-confirms a favored outcome because the cost of self-deception is too high: an embarrassing reputation, estrangement of fellow trekkers, equipment damage, injury, or even death. Such outcomes are often unpredictable, and self-deception merely leaves us less prepared for the unpredictable and increases the severity of the consequences. OKEs keep in check self-deception that damages our epistemology.

OKEs are not exclusively gate-keeping activities that limit self-deception and pretense. OKEs can help build metaphors that guide our life in that they pro-vide a variety of physical experiences that generate metaphorical concepts and language. In a text rich with suggestive power, Mark Johnson argues that we first encounter our physical environment, and detect patterns, such as balance, force, and movement, which we then project onto abstract ideas (Johnson, 1987: xv). We gradually move from the immediate and familiar body patterns to more distant and abstract concepts. For example, we first encounter the concept of balance in a physical way, when we learn to walk, run, and then ride a bicycle. We notice the pattern that might be labeled balance and, after a time, we project our embodied experience into other, more abstract, forms of balance, as in having a balanced bank account, a balanced diet, and balancing our moods (ibid.). Johnson argues further saying, 'because our bodies are very much alike with respect to their physiological make up, we would expect to find commonly shared (if not universal) gestalt structures for many of our physical interactions within our environment' (ibid.: 62). Such shared structures allow us to generalize beyond particular treks and trips and to pursue the insights occasioned by OKEs with the seriousness they deserve. OKEs offer a wide variety of physical experiences that can lay the groundwork for our metaphorical vocabulary. Johnson argues, for example, that we need to encounter force physically before we can know it. OKEs provide first-person, physical experiences with force: the force of gravity in rock climbing, the force of water while kayaking, force of momentum while biking, and the force of the wind in sailing. When we renew, expand, vary, and relearn such physical experiences as force, balance, and movement, we enrich our stock of metaphors which, in turn, offers a vocabulary to understand our experience. OKEs strengthen our grasp of epistemology that forms the basis for knowledge, understanding, and appreciation.

Aesthetics in nature

Many adventurers have stood transfixed by the beauty of a sunset, a rock face, or the sea. They may even endure hardship and cost because they find themselves so magnetically attracted by nature's superabundant beauty. Regular visitors to the outdoors encounter the aesthetic experience of natural beauty with reassuring frequency; such is the bounty of nature.

Nature, however, is not limited to displays of beauty. Nature also allows us to experience the contrasting aesthetics of the sublime and wonder. These aesthetically loaded ideas involve passionate feelings that, perhaps, we encounter all too rarely in the familiar confines of home and office. OKEs can be the media through which we feel the safe fear of the sublime as well as an uplifting sense of wonder. A vigorously physical encounter with nature enhances both sublimity and wonderment.

The naturalist John Muir told of a time in a California forest when he climbed to the topmost reaches of a tree while a mighty storm approached (Muir, 1898: 244–57). If he had not tied himself fast to the tree, the wild buffeting of furious wind against a supple but resistant tree would have thrown him to his death. He experienced the energetic thrill of terror, even though he knew he was safely tied to a tree that was deeply rooted to the earth. Such an experience of safe fear allowed Muir to encounter the sublime. Experiences with wonder, in contrast with sublime, lift us up out of ourselves with something more than pleasure. We lose a sense of self in wonder because the other, the real world outside ourselves, makes itself known in all its majesty, and offers an aesthetic that complements the aesthetic of the sublime. The sublime and wonder energize. They can be found in nature, and OKEs enhance, intensify, and multiply them both. More than wonder, however, the sublime can cause confusion.

Edmund Burke argues that the sublime addresses some of our strongest emotions, such as terror, fear, and astonishment (Burke, 1999: 66–74). Terror may fill our mind, make reason stop, and arrest our movement, but it heightens our sense of the environment because it focuses our attention on something outside us. Terror directs us outside ourselves because dangers in nature are real, and as such, an awareness of terror, a fear of its presence, or feeling astonished at confronting it, may have served us well. Ancestors, who failed to stay alert to the world's terrors, perished. While terror is the source of our attraction toward the sublime, Burke argues the sublime cannot present itself without qualification. In order to appreciate terror it must stand at a proper distance from us, not so close as to threaten our survival but not so far away as to be a mere curiosity. The proper distance is measured by the need to have the sublime hide something, because in obscurity we find danger and doubt. The unknown is fearful and the greater the unknown, the greater the fear. A mountain inspires greater fear than a hill because mountains generally contain more unknown consequences, more things that can threaten us in unpredictable ways, than we find in hills. The same information, e.g. 100 meters, in different settings can hide danger in different ways. 100 meters on level ground inspire no feeling because the view is all too

52 John (Michael) Atherton

familiar. 100 meters upwards may be admired as when we stand at the base of a giant redwood tree. Standing on the edge and looking down into a 100 meter deep crevasse, however, evokes strong emotions because we know not what lurks in the darkness below (ibid.: 72). OKEs provide us with sublime experiences that not only frighten us but also reward us when our mastery of OKEs allows us to step close to danger while we also remain safe from its risk.

Though Burke argues that we find the sublime attractive because we crave strong emotions, the fear engendered in the sublime does not debilitate us. It is not overwhelming in that the terror we feel can be controlled. The sublime experience stops short of a robust threat where our lives are in danger, as when an avalanche crushes everything in its path. In contrast, the sublime feeling of hiking along a windswept saddle between two peaks in a storm may capture our attention, may overwhelm our senses, and may even take us out of ourselves. Even if the storm on the mountain saddle grows fairly forceful, we are, and know ourselves to be, safe; nevertheless, for a limited time we allow ourselves to participate in the real passions of the moment. Such emotions often lie dormant in our lives, and many people desire, on occasion, to revisit them, to stir them up and feel alive in a way that differs from their daily routine.

In addition to the safe terror of the sublime, OKEs open paths to wonder. Socrates says in the *Theatetus* that philosophy begins in wonder (Plato, 1961: 860). Wonder is 'a response to something that has no obvious explanation' (Quinn, 2002: 9). Wonder stands as the mean between the excess of mere curiosity and the defect of dullness. The merely curious person gathers information but fails to appreciate its significance. The dull person, in contrast, avoids gathering in the first place. Wonder is thus the antidote to petty curiosity and dreary dullness.

Philip Fisher offers eight attributes of wonder: sudden, unexpected, rare, sensed all-at-once, first-time experience, feeling of freshness of the world, pleasurable body state, and progress from mystification to explanation (Fisher, 1998: 26). The wonder generated by an OKE may contain all eight attributes, however, only four will be discussed here: rarity, first-time experience, feeling of freshness of the world, and the progression from mystification to explanation.

True wonder is rare. In order to experience wonder, adventurers challenge themselves and seek higher peaks and faster water. Once the adventurer has mastered an OKE, the activity may join the ranks of the familiar. The tamed OKE grows less challenging, and, therefore, becomes less able to inspire wonder. In the continual process of pursuing wonder, the adventurer tries many OKEs. In the process of questing after ever more unusual challenges, adventurers regain the sense that they are engaging in first-time experiences. Even veteran trekkers can renew their excitement and energy. They are learning anew by training for yet another adventure. They are amassing additional skills and insights that open them to new, exciting possibilities. The likelihood of encountering a sense of wonder keeps them youthful and active. The renewed and energized trekker feels a sense of freshness with the world, and feels this freshness all the more keenly because it is one in which the trekker has actively participated. Perhaps the pursuit of wonder is, in itself, a form of wonder that rewards us as we engage in the process.

Fisher's reference to the idea that wonder progresses beyond mystification to explanation resembles Whitehead's rhythms of learning (Whitehead, 1929: 15–28). Whitehead argues that we start with romantic energy, with an excitement that stirs our imagination, makes us giddy, and even, perhaps as Fisher (1998) might say, mystifies us. We maintain this giddiness until we start to ask for details, or what Fisher calls explanations. Soon enough we seek the specifics that will explain the activity that has just a short time ago filled us with romantic energy. Whitehead calls this second stage precision. We pursue precision until romantic energy and precise detail combine to allow us to reach the stage Whitehead calls generalization. In generalization we can stand up and look around because we are already energized and informed. We are now ready to move on. Learning in Whitehead's vision is an ever-renewing cycle, a movement upward to greater insight and wonder.

Wonder and romance both excite our imagination and prompt us to venture forth with energy and expectation. Fisher argues further that 'wonder is the boundary line between the obvious, the ordinary, and the everyday on the one hand, and the unknowable, the inexplicable, and the unfathomable on the other' (Fisher, 1998: 120). OKEs allow us to temporarily leave behind the ordinary and move out toward those activities that may well be inexplicable, or at least impossible to share with those who have not experienced them. Recall the canoeists at the beginning of this chapter and their failed attempt to include an inexperienced person. The claim that you just had to be there suggests we can share wonder with others, but that we need more than just words.

Fisher argues further that when we experience wonder we know that

> [I]t involves a discovery about the limits of the will within experience; a location where we can no longer identify ourselves completely with our powers of choice, actions, self-direction, and yet these territories of experience outside the will are intimately ourselves, uniquely determined, personal. Wonder begins with something imposed on us for thought.
>
> (ibid.: 40)

Fisher's comments on wonder may apply to OKEs when his concepts are appropriately modified to fit an outdoor context. Movement in OKEs must conform to nature's externalities that offer new vistas where we can link thought and perception and, in a sense, unite with them, make them part of our on-going life experience, and integrate the wonder of the OKE with our self.

OKEs can help us get out of ourselves because the path, river, and rock face demand our attention. It is a paradox that in the process of being less self-absorbed, we may come to learn more about the self. Even if we fail to take full advantage of all the aesthetic opportunities found in OKEs, they remain available for reflection at later dates with other trekkers and in different locations. While we may let moments of wonder pass us by because we deny them, are too fatigued, or are otherwise distracted, wonder can alter our thinking and feeling if we remain open to it.

Concluding remarks

The thesis of this chapter is that OKEs affect our epistemology and aesthetic sensitivities. This thesis may need to be qualified lest it seem to present OKEs as a panacea. We know, after all, that not everyone who treks into the backwoods or sails the briny deep returns wide-eyed with philosophic insight. Such is also the case in other human activities. For example, while many people attend museums, theaters, and symphony halls and leave without the experience having had the slightest impact on their lives, such intellectual and experiential imper-meability does not entail that these art venues had nothing to offer. In a similar way, evidence of the philosophic dullness of some wilderness trekkers should not condemn the experience as unworthy of philosophic meditation. Rather, it might be asked how non-standard activities such as rock climbing, canoeing, and hang gliding can help people engage in philosophy.

Consider the following parable.[1] One day a youth sauntered up to Socrates and said he had heard of the revered teacher's reputation for truth and wished to let Socrates teach him. Socrates welcomed the youth and asked him to go on a walk. When they arrived by the water's edge, Socrates knelt by the bank and indicated the youth should join him. He asked the youth what he saw in the water. After the youth's initial reply, Socrates asked him to look closer. Several such exchanges occurred until the youth's nose almost touched the water. Suddenly Socrates grabbed him by the hair and forced his head under water. The more he struggled, the harder Socrates held him down, until, after several flailing minutes, Socrates released the youth, who desperately sucked in the air. Socrates turned the youth to face him and said, 'When you desire to know as much as you want air, then come to see me.'

We too may need a change of venue something like the brief one the smug youth experienced with Socrates. If we are trapped by the tyranny of the familiar, we may need something unusual to shake us up and help us see anew. Outdoor Kinetic Experiences challenge us in ways that force us to reexamine old habits of thought. In so doing, we take new paths to philosophic insight.

Note

1 This well-known story is in keeping with Socrates' character, but I cannot verify its historical accuracy.

References

Adler, M. (1987) 'Teaching, Learning, and Their Counterfeits', in G. Van Doren (ed.) *Reforming Education*, New York: Collier Books.
Armstrong, T. (1993) *7 Kinds of Smart*, New York: Penguin Books.

Burke, E. (1999) 'A Philosophical Inquiry into the Origins of Our Ideas of the Sublime and the Beautiful', in G. Blocker and J. M. Jeffries (eds.) *Contextualizing Aesthetics*, Balmont, CA: Wadsworth.

Casey, E. (2001) 'Between Geography and Philosophy: What Does it Mean to Be in Place-World?' *Annals of the Association of American Geographers*, 91: 683–93.

Dewey, J. (1938) *Experience and Education*, New York: Collier Books.

Fisher, P. (1998) *Wonder, the Rainbow, and the Aesthetic of Wonder*, Cambridge, MA: Harvard University Press.

Gigerenzer, G. (2000) *Adaptive Thinking*, Oxford: Oxford University Press.

Haight, M. R. (1980) *A Study of Self-Deception*, Brighton: Harvester Press.

Johnson, M. (1987) *The Body in the Mind: The Bodily Basics of Meaning*, Chicago: University of Chicago Press.

Muir, J. (1898) 'A Wind-Storm in the Forest', in *The Mountains of California*, New York: Century.

Pieper, J. (1966) *The Four Cardinal Virtues*, Notre Dame, IN: University of Notre Dame Press.

Plato (1961) 'Theatetus', in *Plato, The Collected Dialogues*, ed. E. Hamilton, Princeton, NJ: Princeton University Press.

Polanyi, M. (1966) *The Tacit Dimension*, New York: Doubleday.

Quinn, D. (2002) *Iris Exiled: A Synoptic History of Wonder*, Langham, MD: University Press of America.

Rolston, H. (1997) 'Nature for Real: Is Nature a Social Contract?', in T. D. Chappell (ed.) *The Philosophy of the Environment*, Edinburgh: Edinburgh University Press.

Rousseau, J. J. (1957) *Émile*, trans. B. Foxley, London: J. M. Dent & Sons Ltd.

Rousseau, J. J. (1963) 'The Evils of Education', in R. Gross (ed.) *The Teacher and the Taught*, New York: Dell Pub.

Todd, P. (2001) 'Fast and Frugal Heuristics for Environmentally Bounded Minds', in G. Gigerenzer and R. Selton (eds.) *Bounded Rationality: The Adaptive Toolbox*, Cambridge, MA: MIT Press.

Whitecombe, M. (1998) 'Speech to the Annual Conference of COCEO in Dorset, UK 26 Sept. 1998', available online at http//www3.sympatico.ca.mwhitecombe/OETrans Speech.html, 5 (accessed 31 October 2006).

Whitehead, A. N. (1929) 'The Rhythms of Education', in *The Aims of Education*, New York: The Free Press.

5 Adventure, climbing excellence and the practice of 'bolting'

Philip Ebert and Simon Robertson

In this chapter we examine a recent version of an old controversy within climbing ethics. Our organising topic is the 'bolting' of climbing routes, in particular the increasing bolting of routes in those wilderness areas climbing traditionalists have customarily believed should remain bolt-free. The issues this raises extend beyond the ethical, however, encompassing a wider normative field that concerns individual ideals, the values and goals of different climbing practices and communities, as well as various aesthetic and environmental matters. This makes any assessment of the acceptability of bolting a complex affair, requiring not only the identification of relevant considerations and arguments but also some way to evaluate their comparative significance.

Here, though, we limit our discussion somewhat. We begin by explaining what bolting involves and then introduce some of the general issues it raises by considering as a concrete example disagreements about the acceptability of bolting in what has until recently remained a bastion of the bolt-free ethos – Scottish winter climbing. Second, we examine the roles of excellence and adventure in arguments for and against bolting respectively, concluding that defensible cases can be made on both sides of the debate. Third, we present a new argument for a presumption towards traditional climbing in the Scottish mountains, by implication arguing that the use of bolts should be restricted.

Bolting

Climbing comprises a multifaceted set of practices or games, each with its own methods, styles, goals and ideals.[1] Our focus is on two such games – those that deploy bolts and those that come into conflict with those which deploy bolts. We begin by explaining both 'bolting' and 'bolted climbing'.

Bolting is the practice of drilling into the climbing medium permanent metal rungs, which climbers then use to aid and protect their ascent. A climber clips one karabiner from an 'extender' (usually a short sling attached to two karabiners) onto each bolt reached and places the rope to which he or she is attached through the second karabiner. The climber is belayed by a partner, so that in the event of a fall the climber drops only the distance above the last bolt clipped plus the same distance below the bolt (if 2 metres above a bolt, the climber falls 4 metres in total). Bolted climbing is one form of 'sport climbing'; this being any form of climbing deploying fixed (pre-placed and/or permanent) protection. Because bolted protection is reliable, bolted climbing is relatively safe. With the element of danger reduced, sport routes facilitate climbing at an increased level of technical difficulty, this typically being one of its constitutive aims. What we shall call 'traditional' climbing, in contrast, involves placing one's own protection ('natural protection') to safeguard progression, the second climber on the rope removing it during ascent. Risk is part and parcel of traditional climbing. Not only is the availability of protection often sporadic, the quality of protection is only as good as the climbing medium allows and the climber's skill in placing it. These two factors increase the likely severity of a fall.

In many countries, bolting is an accepted and commonplace practice.[2] In others, like Britain (perhaps especially Scotland), there remains a default presumption against it. Despite this presumption, recent years have seen the development of sport climbing venues on crags and cliffs in Scotland. While many, if not most, traditionalists now at least tolerate established sport venues, they do oppose expanding the repertoire. A recent development they find especially worrying is the creation of sport venues for winter climbing in Scotland.[3] To give a flavour of some of the issues involved in the debate generally, we concentrate on the Scottish case, paying particular attention to the inadequacy of existing legislation.

One of the key issues concerns what would count as a suitable sport climbing venue. In its most recently drafted *Code of Good Practice* (2004), the Mountaineering Council of Scotland (MCoS) accepts 'that there is a place for both sports style and traditional style climbs in the future development of Scottish climbing, both in winter and summer' (Howett, 2004: 13). It suggests nevertheless that bolting be restricted so as to ensure that the 'highly regarded ethos of, and future development of, traditional climbing is not diminished by the development of new sport climbing venues' (ibid.). This seems initially ambiguous: whether the future development of new sport climbing venues is to be restricted on the grounds that it does, in fact, diminish the ethos and development of traditional climbing; or whether it is to be restricted only *if* it were to diminish this highly regarded ethos and development. With respect to the first reading, we can note at least one source of conflict: protagonists of the competing climbing styles sometimes want to climb in the very same area and on the very same cliffs, though traditional climbers typically do not want to climb in areas with a proliferation of bolts. Mark Colyvan expresses the tension thus:

> the proper care of an oval on which football and cricket must coexist is a difficult matter. Unlike the cricket/football problem, though, sport climbers and traditional climbers can not come to some agreement on a temporal demarcation, as both wish to climb all year around and the removal and re-placing of bolts seasonally would not be practical anyway.
>
> (Colyvan, 1993: 20–1)

Given a scarcity of climbing venues within Scotland, we can see that sport climbing does have a damaging effect on the development of traditional climbing, since extensive bolting does, in fact, restrict the space available for the development of further traditional routes.

In order to alleviate such worries, however, the *Code* presents several criteria which it advises 'should be born in mind by climbers when deciding whether a crag is suitable for the production of sports routes in either summer or winter'. (What it is to 'bear in mind' these criteria is far from obvious – one might of course bear them in mind whilst openly flouting their recommendation.) The criteria focus on the 'character' or 'feel' of the prospective venue, for which a number of determinants are offered. The *Code* tells us that:

> The character of a venue is often typified as adventurous (and enhanced) by the wild nature of its surroundings, the imposing nature of the crag, the lack of protection, the seriousness of the approach or descent and the commitment needed from both members of the climbing team.
>
> (Howett, 2004: 13)

In contrast: 'If the potential quality of the route lies in the technical aspects of the climb rather than the stature or adventurous nature then they may give better quality as sport climbs' (ibid.). More specifically, the character of a venue depends on the availability of natural protection, the *Code* advising that 'If there is natural protection available then the route has clearly an adventurous nature and should remain bolt free' (ibid.). Similarly, 'If the crag has strong natural lines, whether some are well protected and others are not, then the character of the crag can be said to be more adventurous and would be best remaining bolt free' (ibid.). The *Code* also suggests that 'Some areas may have a strong local or historical anti-bolt ethic and this should be respected' (ibid.), and that the 'proximity' of a potential 'sport climb to naturally protected climbs' should not be such as to 'detract from the adventurous nature of the latter' – a criterion which, apparently, will 'determine whether currently unclimbed sections of a partially developed crag would be best left for future [traditional] advances' (ibid.).

These descriptions (the 'wild' and 'imposing' nature of a venue, the presence of 'strong natural lines'), as well as the tone of subsequent advice (that some routes '*may* give better quality as sport climbs', that 'a strong local or historical anti-bolt ethic should be *respected*', that some venues 'would be best remaining bolt free'), leave much to interpretation, indeed much to the interpretation of those with vested interests in precisely these practices. We should not expect an exact science when it comes to deciding on the suitability of a venue for one or other style of climbing. Yet the *Code* is not sufficiently explicit even to guide good practice in a context where most parties would quite reasonably hope to be offered a clear conclusion – the acceptability of bolts in the mountains. It ambivalently declares that 'Under *most* circumstances the placing of bolts is inappropriate on mountain cliffs . . . *but there may be exceptions*' (Howett, 2004: 13, our emphasis). Instructions that explicitly permit exceptions yet fail to clarify what exceptions are acceptable do little – so the proponent of traditional climbing will fear – to protect the traditional ethos and its development.

Furthermore, the criteria offered in the *Code* quite easily permit conflict. On the one hand, the *Code* allows that bolting be permitted on routes lacking natural protection; on the other, it seems to want to restrict bolting to 'low-lying inland crags' – the obvious thought being that some relatively high-level lines in mountainous areas lack natural protection.[4] Similarly, the *Code* claims that sea-cliffs should generally remain bolt-free; yet some sea-cliffs are not suitable for natural protection and so satisfy one of the *Code*'s criteria for the acceptability of bolting, while also satisfying one criterion for remaining bolt-free. What to do in such circumstances is left open by the *Code* and no further criteria are given to provide practical guidance in these cases.[5]

This lack of specificity in turn gives rise to a further worry, namely that bolting, even on low-lying naturally unprotected crags, leads down a slippery slope to a more pervasive bolting culture. Though we are not wholeheartedly condoning slippery-slope *reasoning*, the recent developments of winter sport venues to which we refer do at least indicate that such worries are not *in practice* unfounded.[6]

So far we have attempted to show that there is a genuine practical conflict between sport climbing and traditional climbing (one which current legislation does little to allay). A full examination of the conflict requires a wide-ranging discussion to which a single chapter could not do justice. But having introduced some of the issues, we now consider the role of two values in climbing, excellence and adventure, our aim being twofold: to assess what we believe to be the strongest arguments for and against bolting, and to diagnose perhaps the main source at the heart of the conflict between those on each side of the debate.

A perfectionist argument

For many, climbing provides opportunity to escape from the perceived mundanity and petty rules of day-to-day life. It offers a degree of freedom from the externally imposed duties and expectations that constrain us in societal life, freedom to pursue our own personal projects in a way unfettered by those constraints. The nature of the projects we do pursue of course shapes and structures how we are able to express such freedom; but given the ethos of freedom which climbing seems to offer, it might in turn be supposed that climbing not only permits individual expression but that it falls beyond the jurisdiction of *any* juridical authority or mandate. As a result, one may be tempted to conclude that if *I* want to bolt routes as part of *my* personal project, that is what *I* am permitted or even entitled to do (or, more interestingly, the issue of permission never even arises). There are a number of obvious worries with such an argument. For one thing, even if one's climbing projects are themselves neither morally perverse nor impermissible with respect to state law, this does not show that they fall outside the jurisdiction of all ethical constraint. The climbing world has its own governing bodies, one role of which is to implement 'rules' that guide and sometimes check practices in a way that protects the freedoms required for others to pursue their projects. The authority of such bodies may itself be open to dispute; but the issue remains as to whether the practices they rule against are practices one ought not engage in. And insofar as it is plausible to assume that not all climbing practices are acceptable, the question is whether bolting in particular is. To assess this, we need to show that bolting is something climbers have (good enough) reason to do.

We think the strongest pro-bolting argument lies in the suggestion that sport climbing is valuable in virtue of its facilitating the advancing of climbing standards amongst elite climbers. Because sport climbing is pre-protected and relatively safe, it allows climbers to move safely at the limit of their capabilities on routes they would be unable or unwilling to attempt with the less reliable protection traditional climbing affords (the limits in question typically concerning those of technique, strength and endurance). Climbing harder in turn improves the climber's abilities, fostering the qualities necessary not just to improve their own climbing but also, for those at the top end of the sport, to surpass existing levels of achievement by other climbers. Insofar as technical advances are valuable in their own right, or at least insofar as the kinds of excellence required to make such advances are valuable, the value of sport climbing that makes this possible provides (at least some) reason to allow it. We shall call this the 'perfectionist' argument since it seeks to justify sport climbing by its role in the development of climbing excellence at the elite end of the activity. We develop this argument in the rest of the present section.

An obvious assumption underwriting the argument is that climbing excellence is a valuable or worthwhile aim, at least relative to what is valuable about climbing. While we cannot defend the claim fully here, we find it plausible that, just as the goals of climbing in its various forms are shaped by the climbing community and the climbers that comprise it, the values of climbing are shaped by standards internal to those practices and the climbing community. And one of these values is excellence. Certainly, climbers themselves value improving their own abilities, to which end they challenge themselves with progressively more testing climbs; and those within the climbing community typically regard as admirable those climbers who surpass existing standards of climbing excellence by pushing further the limits of achievement.[7] To this extent, we shall assume that excellence is one value of climbing.

An immediate complication emerges, though. Different climbing games, including sport and traditional climbing, each have their own internal standards by which excellence is measured; and what counts as excellence relative to the standards of one climbing game may not count as valuable by the standards of another. Traditional climbers, for example, may value the development of standards in traditional climbing yet, if they deride the value of sport climbing, regard its technical advances as valueless. Pro-bolters therefore require an additional assumption if they are to defend the value of bolting in such a way that does not turn solely upon their own pro-bolting preferences (preferences whose value may be in doubt). One way to do this is to show that the advances made through sport climbing are transferable in that they serve to improve the standards of difficulty and excellence achievable on traditional routes. This would demonstrate not only that excellence in sport climbing is valuable with respect to the goals internal to sport climbing, but that such excellence is valuable for traditional climbing too. If they can show this, then even the sport-antagonistic traditionalist, who values developments at the cutting edge of traditional climbing, has reason to value (advances made in) sport climbing. Whether or not these skills are transferable is an empirical matter. With rock climbing, the evidence indicates that they are: not only have standards in traditional climbing advanced in tandem with the progression of standards in sport climbing, the vast majority of the best traditional climbers train on sport routes precisely to develop their technical abilities, power and endurance. With winter climbing, matters are less clear. One view is that winter climbing at the cutting edge requires certain heightened psychological qualities that only experience of leading winter routes traditional style can bring. While any form of climbing requires of the climber a degree of mental control in the face of physical insecurity, the especially insecure terrain and unreliable protection typical of extreme winter climbing requires a level of mental control exceeding that which could be provided through sport climbing. In defence of the perfectionist argument, however, we should note that the plausibility of this objection trades on the assumption that those doing sport routes in order to improve their traditional winter climbing abilities do not already possess, to a suitable degree, the psychological qualities in question. Even if practising winter sport climbs would not by itself cultivate the skills necessary to succeed at the forefront of traditional winter climbing, by combining the technical benefits of winter sport climbing with their existing experience on hard traditional routes, climbers would improve on the latter. In which case, at least for those already at the cutting edge of traditional winter climbing, the availability of sport routes may well support improvements in traditional climbing after all.

We want to consider two lines of objection to the argument so far, responses to which will serve to constrain its general application. The underlying claim of the perfectionist argument is that sport climbing, in either summer or winter conditions, is *instrumentally* valuable, valuable as a means to improving climbing standards and excellence. A first line of objection is that climbers who create and climb bolted routes, perhaps especially winter sport routes, regard sport climbing as a valuable end in its own right but *not* as a means to the development of standards in traditional climbing. This worry has two aspects. First, one might think that if climbers do not use sport routes as a means to develop their technical ability for traditional climbing, the perfectionist justification for the creation of sport venues, which relies on their being instrumentally valuable, fails. It would fail because the argument goes through only if sport climbing actually has the effect to which it is supposedly a means. (This may be a particularly pressing concern in the present context of Scottish winter climbing, where those currently at the cutting edge of traditional climbing seem reluctant to use winter sport routes as a means.) This raises a number of complications both theoretical and practical, given that the creation of a sport route might prove justified only retrospectively, whereas we want to know whether it is now justifiable. Nonetheless, for practical purposes at least, the following line of response to this worry offers a relatively commonsense reply: if bolting is to be acceptable on perfectionist grounds, those intending to develop sport climbing venues must at least have sufficient reason to believe that such venues will in practice facilitate improved standards at the forefront of traditional climbing. A lot more would need to be said to vindicate this suggestion fully on theoretical grounds. Nevertheless, insofar as it presents a plausible line of response, we now turn to the second aspect of the objection.

The second aspect of the worry is that the actions of somebody who appeals to the perfectionist argument to justify bolting, but who regards sport climbing as an end in its own right and not also as valuable with respect to traditional climbing, would not be justified in bolting. For the perfectionist argument we have presented requires that the justification for sport climbing is grounded just in the advancements it makes possible for traditional climbing. Not only might the motivations of someone who appeals to the perfectionist argument to justify bolts, but whose real goal lies elsewhere, be somewhat infelicitous, more significantly their actions would not be prospectively justified by the perfectionist argument to which they appeal, since the reasons for which they bolt are not the reasons sanctioned by the perfectionist argument. Together, these two aspects of the overall objection suggest that the perfectionist argument will work only if those who develop sport climbing venues have sufficient reason to believe that such venues will benefit traditional climbers *and* they sincerely intend this effect.

A further objection, however, may be raised. Even if sport climbing is instrumentally valuable, in the sense that it serves as *one* means to improvements in standards for traditional climbing, it does not seem to be a *necessary* means. There are, after all, other ways to develop climbing standards – with indoor climbing walls, bouldering, and so on. In which case, the perfectionist argument appears weakened, at the very least placing the onus on those who favour bolting to provide further argument to demonstrate its acceptability.

The most promising response, we think, is to show that although (outdoor) sport climbing is not the only available means to the advancement of climbing standards, it is nevertheless the best means. Indeed, it is plausible to suppose that climbing on real rock or mixed routes of technical severity similar to or surpassing the standards set at the upper echelon of traditional climbing is the most effective form of technical training. Although there may be other ways to develop general strength, for example, the specific kinds of power, endurance and technical skills required for extreme climbing are most effectively developed through climbing itself. Granting that this is so, the perfectionist argument, incorporating the earlier caveats, seems to us defensible. Nonetheless, we should emphasise the limitations of the argument. It does not by itself show that bolting is acceptable. Rather, it provides part of an explanation for why, if bolting is acceptable, it is so. For even if bolting is the best means to developing climbing excellence on traditional routes, the question remains whether that means is itself justifiable.

We have been implicitly assuming, for sake of simplicity, that the end of excellence would justify sport climbing instrumentally; yet we have not ruled out the possibility that, despite its instrumental value, other considerations might render it unacceptable. So we think that, while the argument itself is defensible, by itself it yields at best a *prima facie* case for bolting, a fuller assessment of its acceptability requiring consideration of other reasons for and against the practice. In the next section, we introduce a set of arguments against bolting which emerge from considering the role of adventure in climbing.

Adventure

It is sometimes suggested, by climbing traditionalists, that in those areas where traditional styles of climbing are the norm, that norm itself supplies a default presumption against bolting. By itself this suggestion is inadequate if intended to justify prohibition; for the very issue is precisely whether the tradition reflected by that norm is a tradition worth defending. To assess this, we need to consider what it is about traditional climbing that is of value and then see how this might form part of an argument against bolting. We focus on one of the central values of traditional climbing – adventure. We first analyse the conception of adventure integral to traditional climbing, and then go on to examine the extent to which bolted climbing lacks adventure before evaluating how this contributes to a case against bolting.

The precise extent to which we think of climbing as adventurous depends on many factors, including not only the nature of the climb itself and the style of ascent deployed, but also its location. Our primary focus is climbing in mountain regions or other remote wilderness areas. In what sense, then, is traditional climbing in such areas to be thought of as adventurous? We begin by distinguishing two relevant components: exploration and risk.

The exploratory nature and value of traditional climbing has two main elements. On the one hand, there remains the possibility to discover new climbing routes, either by finding cliffs not previously explored or by exploring the potential for new climbs at more established venues. For many, a principal attraction of climbing is being in remote areas, areas where the climber is more likely to be alone – not just far from the madding crowds of other climbers all attempting (sometimes clogging up) the same route, but being able to enjoy the solitude itself. Exploratory climbing of this type serves those who desire remoteness. On the other hand, the process of climbing, whether pioneering a new route or repeating an established one, can itself be an exploratory process, one that involves route-finding, the assessment of alternative lines, finding suitable placements for protection, and so forth. Again, for many this is a fundamental attraction of climbing.

The other component of adventure comes from the fact that traditional climbing is dangerous (at least potentially) and thus typically involves an element of personal risk. While part of the appeal of traditional climbing is the risk involved, the climber typically seeks to diminish the danger and risk to an 'acceptable level', though without removing it entirely. Climbers do not generally climb under the description *doing something dangerous* but, rather, *overcoming the dangers inherent to the activity*, the aim being to control both the physical danger and one's reactions to it.[8] Although climbers know that injury and death are possibilities, they do not *intend* them, nor climb because it increases their probabilities. Climbing in remote areas is especially committing in that it heightens risk by magnifying the significance – the likely impact and effect – of mistakes. This idea of commitment has both a physical and psychological dimension. Physically, the risks involved in climbing in remote areas are greater, the event of injury typically requiring both greater self-reliance and effort to return safe, the success of self-rescue less assured. The climber of course knows this, his or her awareness of it adding an important psychological dynamic to the activity: not only can the feeling of risk, occurrent or underlying, be more intense, the degree of focus and mental toughness required to execute the climb is to that extent greater, with the success of achievement in turn more gratifying.

When combined with the kinds of gratification climbers experience upon moving fluently over their medium or else struggling to overcome its obstacles, the exploratory and risk dimensions of traditional climbing contribute to an aesthetic experience of sorts, at least for those suitably disposed.[9] With bolted climbing, however, certain elements of exploration and risk are either lessened or eradicated entirely, and traditional climbers often remark on how comparatively empty the experience of sport climbing is, even if it sometimes allows for more fluid movement and progression over rock.[10] So in what ways is sport climbing 'less adventurous'?

On the one hand, there is nothing to stop the sport climber from exploring remote areas and pioneering new (bolted) routes on previously unclimbed lines. Nonetheless, sport climbing is less explorative in two main ways. First, if the bolter climbing a new (previously unbolted) route faces a difficult section from which the traditional climber would retreat, he or she may simply drill a bolt, thereby either removing the obstacle or making it protected and thus safer.[11] Second, once bolts are in place and a bolted route exists, this removes the exploratory element of route finding, since one just follows the line of metal.[12] One could of course explore ways of linking different bolted routes on the same face, so long as those routes are free of other climbers. Notwithstanding this, not only is this 'exploration' constrained by the availability of pre-placed bolts, the prevalence of bolts itself makes the climbing less adventurous by removing both the physical risk and a sense of what climbers often refer to as 'being out there on the sharp end of the rope'. Although it is possible that those committed to traditional tactics climb a sport line without using the bolts on it, not only would there be a constant reminder of the kind of item to which they object; the very presence of bolts, with the added security it offers, changes the nature of both the activity and experience. Climbing in such conditions is less committing, in terms of both the seriousness of the activity and the attitudes thereby required of the climber. For the climber would know that if he or she hits difficulty, reliable protection and/or a pre-established means of escape lie in wait. In these ways, bolted routes lack the adventure which many think is paramount to climbing itself.

We want now to examine three related arguments against bolting which the appeal to adventure might support. Each is successively less robust in terms of the substantive conclusions they seek to justify, though in turn more defensible. The first argument runs as follows: climbing is by nature (e.g. essentially) adventurous. If this is the case then climbing is valuable to the extent that it is adventurous. As bolted climbing is not adventurous, it cannot therefore be valuable.[13] There are a number of obvious problems with this argument. One worry is that it relies on the (disputable) assumption that bolted climbing cannot be adventurous in any respect. Under this view, sport 'climbing' is not actually climbing – since if adventure is an essential part of climbing, and if bolted climbing lacks the relevant sense of adventure, then it lacks a feature an activity must have if it is to count as climbing. This position is unsustainable. Insofar as those who use bolts are making movements identical in type to those made by traditional climbers, it is difficult to see why the use of fixed rather than natural protection renders the ascent something other than a climb.

Perhaps, though, we might just remove the problematic first premise, revising the argument as follows: climbing is valuable to the extent that it is adventurous; bolted climbing is not adventurous; so bolted climbing is not valuable. Even so, the argument is problematic. It is worth drawing attention, first, to the phrase in the first premise 'to the extent that', which is ambiguous. On the one hand, it might mean that climbing is valuable *only if* adventurous; but this is a strong claim, which rules out the possibility that climbing could be a valuable or worthwhile activity in respect of features other than adventure unless it is at the same time adventurous (as we might put it: its being adventurous would *uniformly* have to serve as both *the* value-providing feature *and* a feature whose presence *enables* any other feature to have value).[14] We find it hard to see how an argument for this could be given. On the other hand, the locution 'to the extent that' might imply that climbing is valuable *in proportion* to the degree of adventure it involves. There is a weaker and a stronger version of this claim. The stronger version is that the value of climbing is determined *solely* by the degree to which it is adventurous. Yet this is again too strong since it excludes the possibility that climbing is ever valuable in respects other than adventure. Furthermore, it implies that the more adventurous (e.g. dangerous or risky) a climb, the more valuable it is – whereas we would generally expect there to be some rough threshold of danger or risk beyond which the value of a climb diminishes (one only has to think of climbs that turn into (near-) disaster scenarios). The weaker version of the claim is that the more adventurous a climb is the more valuable it is *qua adventure*, at least once possible thresholds at which value diminishes are factored in. This allows that climbing can be valuable in virtue of features other than adventure and that those other features can contribute to its overall value. Note that the second premise of the argument – that bolting is not adventurous – is not something we have argued for; nor are we denying that bolting can be adventurous, or that it can be valuable in further respects. What the anti-bolting argument has to say, though, is that traditional climbing is more valuable than bolted climbing *with respect to adventure.*

These considerations take us on to the third and, to our mind, most plausible of the arguments from adventure against bolting. It runs as follows: traditional climbing is more adventurous than bolted climbing; so, traditional climbing is more valuable than bolted climbing with respect to adventure. Obviously this relies on the suppressed premise that adventure, or at least adventurous climbing, is valuable. We shall not here question whether adventure itself is or can be valuable but shall take it for granted. Insofar as climbing is adventurous, then, it is or can be valuable. The phrase 'is valuable' in this context means something like 'is worthwhile' and it should be uncontroversial that traditional climbing is, in respect of adventure, a more worthwhile activity than bolted climbing – in the sense that traditional climbing is generally more conducive to an exploratory experience involving risk, with adventure generally being partly constitutive of the value of traditional climbing. We should nonetheless add a proviso here, to the effect that a traditional route is typically more adventurous than a sport route *of similar technical standard.* We are not committed to the view that bolted climbing is never as adventurous as traditional climbing (nor, therefore, that bolted climbing cannot be adventurous in some ways and to some degree); we make the weaker claim that, generally, traditional climbing is more adventurous, and therein valuable with respect to adventure, than bolted climbing.[15]

We find this third argument quite plausible; and few climbers would deny that, in respect of adventure, traditional climbing offers more than bolted climbing. Yet we also acknowledge its limitations. It presents only one way in which traditional climbing is more valuable than sport climbing, with there being many further considerations relevant to a proper assessment of the acceptability of bolting. In the following section we therefore develop a further line of argument in favour of traditional climbing – and, by implication, against bolted routes in the mountains.

An argument for the traditional ethos

The argument we advance in this section relies on the idea that valuable activities typically have certain preconditions that have to be in place for the valuable activity to be realisable. Insofar as there is a good reason to respect the valuable activity itself there will also be some reason to preserve the relevant preconditions. The mode of reasoning that underlies this argument is often found in so-called 'closure-reasoning' in epistemology. We briefly explain the idea behind 'closure-reasoning' and then transfer that idea to the evaluative context.

The idea is that knowledge is closed under known entailment. If you know that *p*, and if you know that *if p then q*, then you know or are in a position to know that *q*. For example, if you know that *it's snowing on the Buchaille Etive Mor* and you know that *if it's snowing on the Buchaille Etive Mor then it's snowing in Glen Coe*, you know or are in a position to know that *it's snowing in Glen Coe*.

Most epistemologists accept (some version of) a closure principle; we shall now explore how a similar style of reasoning, in an evaluative context, would support anti-bolting intuitions.

First, let us assume that traditional climbing is valuable and that one way it is so is by virtue of its being adventurous. Now for the value of climbing qua adventure to be realisable, certain conditions must obtain: in particular, there have to be suitably remote traditional climbing venues free from bolts. As an intermediate conclusion, we may say that the relevant realisability conditions for climbing being of value (by virtue of its being adventurous) are themselves valuable. This is the rough analogue of the closure reasoning about knowledge, here applied to the notion of value. The most plausible way in which such conditions are valuable is extrinsic[16] – the value of the mountains being bolt-free depends on the value of adventurous climbing. Now if two valuable courses of action are incompatible with one another in that the realisation of the value of either one excludes the realisation of the value of the other, the more valuable course of action is the one we have more reason to promote (to protect and/or pursue). In which case, given that on any climbing venue the realisability of the value of traditional climbing *qua its being adventurous* is incompatible with there being sport routes, then assuming that the value of adventure that is part of traditional climbing makes it more valuable than sport climbing, there is a presumption in favour of traditional climbing and thus against sport climbing.

This argument clearly depends on the assumption that the value of adventure that is part of traditional climbing does make it more valuable than sport climbing. Although we have not argued directly for this, it is eminently plausible. For one thing, many sport climbers agree that traditional climbing is a purer and in some sense superior form of climbing to sport climbing. Furthermore, the perfectionist argument *for bolting* that we discussed in the previous section implicitly rests on the claim that the value of sport climbing *derives from* the value of traditional climbing to which it is a means – arguably suggesting that traditional climbing is the ultimately valuable form of climbing. We should add, however, that this reasoning, if defensible, generates only a *prima facie* presumption in favour of traditional climbing, one that may be overridden once other factors about the respective values of the two forms of climbing are factored in. Nevertheless, the argument places the onus on bolters to justify further development of sports venues, for if there is a presumption in favour of traditional climbing in adventurous climbing venues and thereby against sport climbing, the default presumption against bolting remains intact. Much more would need to be said in order to assess the ultimate cogency of the argument. An initial worry with the argument, as it stands, might be that analogous reasoning could be applied in defence of bolting. Insofar as any such argument would have to show that sport climbing is a more valuable or worthwhile activity than traditional climbing, we remain sceptical about its prospects.

If our argument is sound then it leads to the elevation of traditional climbing over sports climbing. It would thus call for serious revisions in the *Code of Practice* we criticised earlier; and it may provide the basis for a more instructive and practically informative code which protects the traditional climbing ethos the *Code* claims to represent.[17] Let us stress again, however, that the argument as stated requires further consideration; we leave it in the hope that it presents food for further thought.

Conclusion

In this chapter we have discussed what we regard as the strongest arguments for and against bolting. These arguments focus on the pursuit of two different values – of excellence and of adventure – which underlie sport and traditional climbing respectively. We have shown that, though both arguments are defensible, they do not by themselves conclusively justify or forbid the use of bolts. The considerations in favour of the use of bolts in the second section provided a *prima facie* case for bolting, though without thereby justifying its use on all climbing venues. In contrast, the argument in the last section is best understood as providing a presumption in favour of traditional climbing at specifically adventurous climbing venues. There are of course other considerations relevant to a full assessment of the acceptability of bolting. Nevertheless, we hope that this chapter has helped to illuminate the disagreement about bolting by both connecting it to the values underlying the respective activities and identifying some of the arguments that can be advanced on each side.

Notes

1 See Tejada-Flores (1978) for classic discussion of these different games and the contrasting ideals they represent.
2 In many continental European countries it is the decision of the first ascencionist whether to place bolts instead of natural protection. For classic discussions of bolting in America (especially Yosemite), see the pieces by Robbins (1978), Harding (1978), Chouinard (1978), Drasdo (1978), each reprinted in Wilson (1978).
3 We have in mind Beinn Udlaidh (near Crianlarich), a reliable ice-climbing venue at an altitude of 850 metres, whose lower tier was bolted in 2004–5 for the purpose of training in relative safety for traditional winter climbing. For heated discussion amongst leading climbers, see for example the online climbing forums www.ukclimbing.com and www.scottishclimbs.com. In what follows, we use the description 'winter climbing' to include those forms of ice and mixed climbing (the latter on a possible combination of snow, ice, rock, frozen turf and the like) involving the use of specialist winter equipment such as ice axes and crampons.
4 The still contentious bolting in the early 1980s of unprotected lines in between some classic traditional routes at Creag a Bhancair (on Glen Coe's famous Buachaille Etive Mor) gives a concrete example of the kinds of conflict the *Code* leaves open. One explanation for the lack of clarity of the *Code* might be that it seeks to accommodate (and so legitimate) the continued use of this and other bolted venues.
5 The bolting of the Arbroath sea-cliffs was initially regarded as contentious but it has now become a more or less accepted sport climbing venue.
6 For more on slippery slope arguments, see for example Williams (1995).
7 Our thought here is analogous to Mill's claim that the only evidence for something being desirable is that people desire it (Mill, 1993: 36 [*Utilitarianism* ch. 4.3]); likewise, the only (or at least best) evidence that climbing excellence is valuable is that climbers value it.

8 The idea of overcoming dangers by controlling them is a recurring theme in climbing literature. See for example the interviews with Reinhold Messner, Walter Bonatti, Royal Robbins, Votek Kurtyka and Tomo Cesen in O'Connell (1993).

9 Interestingly, the vast literature on aesthetic experience typically focuses on the experience of the spectator rather than that of the performer. For some recent debate on what it is to have an aesthetic experience, see Carroll (2006) and Iseminger (2006).

10 In correspondence, the Scottish climber Alastair Robertson suggests that 'Sport climbing is the equivalent of McDonald's compared with Haute Cuisine. It tastes good initially but is quickly forgotten and you are left with a certain emptiness soon afterwards. That said, I quite enjoy going to McDonald's on occasion and it makes me further appreciate a fine dish!!'

11 Messner (1978) famously objects to bolting on exactly these grounds, claiming that it involves 'murdering the impossible'. A further consideration relevant in this context is the possibility that future climbers may be able to climb a sports route without bolts, due to which, it is sometimes claimed, bolts should not have been deployed in the first place and/or we have a responsibility to protect potential future climbing lines for future generations. This raises a number of interesting issues that we cannot pursue here.

12 There are also broadly aesthetic-environmental considerations relevant here – for many climbers, the very sight of metal (or other manmade items) on rock faces detracts from the beauty of the face and thereby spoils the aesthetic experience itself.

13 Messner (in O'Connell, 1993: 22) suggests something like this.

14 For more on enabling conditions, mainly in the context of normative reasons for action, see Dancy (2004: ch. 3).

15 The rider 'generally' need not be understood purely statistically. See for example Dreier (1990).

16 In roughly the sense intended by Korsgaard (1983).

17 This new *Code* might well render previous bolting venues illegitimate despite its current acceptance. We think that this is a bullet one may have to bite if, as pay-off, a clearer and more precise guide for *future* practice is gained.

References

Carroll, N. (2006) 'Aesthetic Experience: A Question of Content', in M. Kieran (ed.), *Contemporary Debates in Aesthetics and the Philosophy of Art*, Oxford: Blackwell.

Chouinard, Y. (1978) 'Coonyard Mouths Off', in K. Wilson (ed.), *Games Climbers Play*, London: Bâton Wicks.

Colyvan, M. (1993) 'Ethics, Morality and Rockclimbing', *T.H.E.* 6: 20–1, reprinted in *Screamer* (1993) 52: 3–5, and in *Redpoint* (1993) 14: 4.

Dancy, J. (2004) *Ethics Without Principles*, Oxford: Clarendon Press.

Drasdo, H. (1978) 'A Climb in Cae Coch Quarry', in K. Wilson (ed.), *Games Climbers Play*, London: Bâton Wicks.

Dreier, J. (1990) 'Internalism and Speaker Relativism', *Ethics*, 101: 6–26.

Harding, P. (1978) 'A Meeting with Dolphin', in K. Wilson (ed.), *Games Climbers Play*, London: Bâton Wicks.

Howett, K. (2004) 'The Code of Practice for Scottish Sports Climbing', *The Scottish Mountaineer*, 25: 13.

Iseminger, G. (2006) 'The Aesthetic State of Mind', in M. Kieran (ed.), *Contemporary Debates in Aesthetics and the Philosophy of Art*, Oxford: Blackwell.

Korsgaard, C. (1983) 'Two Distinctions in Goodness', *Philosophical Review*, 92: 169–96.

Messner, R. (1978) 'Murder of the Impossible', in K. Wilson (ed.), *Games Climbers Play*, London: Bâton Wicks.

Mill, J. S. (1993) *Utilitarianism, On Liberty, Considerations on Representative Government, Remarks on Bentham's Philosophy*, ed. G. Williams, London: Everyman.

O'Connell, N. (1993) *Beyond Risk: Conversations With Climbers*, London: Diadem Books.

Robbins, R. (1978) 'Tis-Sa-Sack', in K. Wilson (ed.), *Games Climbers Play*, London: Bâton Wicks.

Tejada-Flores, L. (1978) 'Games Climbers Play', in K. Wilson (ed.), *Games Climbers Play*, London: Bâton Wicks.

Williams, B. (1995) 'Which Slopes are Slippery?', reprinted in B. Williams, *Making Sense of Humanity*, Cambridge: Cambridge University Press.

Wilson, K. (ed.) (1978) *The Games Climbers Play*, London: Bâton Wicks.

6 Reading water

Risk, intuition, and insight

Douglas Anderson

Henri Bergson says that 'the philosopher neither obeys nor commands; he seeks to be at one with nature' (Bergson, 1968: 149). Duke Kahanamoku, father of modern surfing, reflecting on his practice, remarked: 'You are rewarded with a feeling of complete freedom and independence when rocketing across the face of a wave' (Kahanamoku, 1968: 94). There is a strong affinity between Bergson's description of philosophical practice and the reading of water that lies at the heart of extreme surfing and whitewater paddling. Extreme surfers seek giant waves, often being towed out to offshore sites where waves run between 40 and 60 feet. The extreme paddlers to whom I will refer are not those who negotiate waterfalls but those who routinely seek to paddle whitewater that is rated at the top end of or above the current rating system. This affinity between philosophical practice and reading water is twofold. On the one hand, both the surfer and paddler engage in a perceptual endeavor akin to what Bergson requires of the philosopher. On the other hand, both the extreme water athlete and the Bergsonian philosopher achieve a way of being in the world that is natural but not ordinary.

For Bergson, as for William James, perception is not the externalized act of receiving sense impressions so often described by the tradition of British empiricism. It is rather an ability to be with things in the world in such a way that one comes to see the world from their perspective. It is in this sense that the perceiver becomes one with its object. Extreme surfers and paddlers often talk as if they experience something very much like this kind of Bergsonian perception or intuition, and the first section of the chapter will deal with building this analogy by providing an exposition of Bergson's and William James's notions of perceiving and comparing this to what some extreme athletes have to say about how they 'read' the water that carries them. In the second section of the chapter, I will turn to the effects of such perceiving. I will suggest that the reading of water can lead to experiences some will describe as transformative, mystical, or spiritual. And I will point out that, to Bergson and James, this is not a mystery but a very natural feature of human existence, albeit one that must be worked for and developed. Such 'seeing' or 'reading' involves a kind of disengagement from the ordinary way of looking at things and a willingness to risk oneself. If Bergson and James are right, then, extreme surfing and paddling may be especially appropriate practices for 'being alive,' for gaining something like spiritual insight. This makes them analogous to, if not in some ways identical with, philosophy. Philosophy is a kind of 'seeing' for Bergson, and those capable of reading water are especially adept seers; they have an ability to disengage the mind or, as James puts it, to be in 'the aboriginal flow of feeling' (James, 1919: 95).[1] We might say that both of these practices are 'extremely' human and humanizing, yielding the possibility of insight into what James calls 'the significance of life.'

The risking situation

Living tamely has a tendency to give the upper hand in our existence to the understanding or what Immanuel Kant might have described as a mechanical knowing of ourselves and our worlds. We calculate the odds, we predict outcomes, we play by the percentages – we are bettors, but we are not gamblers in such a situation. As Michael Ventimiglia puts it, if you are a bettor, 'you lack the faith in yourself necessary to risk what you have for what you want' (Ventimiglia, 2006: 168). In 'On What Makes Life Significant,' William James recalls his experience at a summer retreat in Chautauqua, NY. It was a beautiful but tame world – a 'middle-class paradise without a sin, without a victim, without a blot, without a tear' (James, 1910: 270). In it he felt something was amiss, and on his return to the 'outer' world, he understood that what he was missing was life's sense of 'precipitousness' or risk. James's concern is a bit startling and is worth reading at length:

> This order is too tame, this culture too second rate, this goodness too uninspiring. This human drama without a villain or a pang; this community so refined that ice-cream soda-water is the utmost offering it can make to the brute animal in man; this city simmering in the tepid lakeside sun; this atrocious harmlessness of all things, – I cannot abide with them. Let me take my chances in the big outside worldly wilderness with all its sins and sufferings. There are the heights and depths, the precipices and the steep ideals, the gleams of the awful and the infinite; and there is more hope and help a thousand times than in this dead level and quintessence of every mediocrity.
>
> (ibid.)

Chautauqua was a mini-Enlightenment Utopia where good reason governed life and everything was safe and predictable. In this sort of world, Bergson and James suggest, the mind employs concepts and categories to organize and control its environment. Concepts provide ways of

> *handling* the perceptual flux and *meeting* distant parts of it; and as far as this primary function of conception goes, we can only conclude it to be . . . a faculty superadded to our barely perceptual consciousness for its use in practically adapting us to a larger environment . . .
>
> (James, 1919: 65–6)

As James suggests, this overly intellectual way of considering the world can become inverted – the intellectualist gives primacy to concepts over the experiential world they were meant to explain. As Bergson remarks, 'Not with impunity, either, can we congeal into distinct and independent things the fluidity of a continuous undivided process' (Bergson, 1959: 114). Both James and Bergson call for us to move into, or at least not to lose sight of, the existentially more real world of risk – a world in which loss is a real possibility – and to revert to a more intuitive and perceptual way of dealing with our world. Risk demands better perception; we need to attend to nature's dynamism and its attendant note of contingency. We need both to risk losing our constructed tame world and to see the risks inherent in a nature that is thoroughly and relentlessly dynamic. Only then will we know or be acquainted with the world in its full actuality. Both James and Bergson believed we are capable of such a reversion:

> But the truth is that our mind is able to follow the reverse procedure. It can be installed in the mobile reality, adopt its ceaselessly changing direction, in short, grasp it intuitively. But to do that, it must do itself violence, reverse the direction by which it ordinarily thinks, continually upsetting its categories, or rather, recasting them.
>
> (Bergson, 1968: 224)

Those who engage in extreme surfing and whitewater paddling know experientially the force of such a reversal. They know that no simple categorical or conceptual analysis will suffice to finish riding a wave or a rapid. Pierre de Villiers, one of South Africa's eminent big wave surfers, describes this sort of inversion in his own experiences reading water on big waves at Dungeons:

> I think everything else is blocked out at that point, you're very single minded. Everything's happening so fast, but at the same time it's kind of like slow motion, you're dropping down and there are so many situations coming at you, there's bits of chop on the face, or there's a bit of a ledge that's come up from a rock underneath, the wave's changing all the time, it seems like time has expanded. Time gets expanded and you're noticing little bits of kelp floating up the wave, or people on the side of you, you tend to notice small things that seem to take a long time and you're adjusting to the situation all the time, you're changing the track of your board or setting an edge a little harder, to do the things that are going to take you out of that situation again.
>
> (Weaver, 2002: 4–5)

De Villiers, like other extreme water athletes, understands inserting oneself into the presence of 'mobile reality' and he is well attuned to its risks. Some suggest that these are the very reasons athletes engage in these extreme practices. Brought alive by the risk, the precipitousness, the precariousness of the situation, they get to see – to know – the world in ways that others do not. The reading of the water is an act of perception that both is a gateway into the presence of mobile reality and, at the same time, reveals to them what is significant in being humanly alive. But this hinges on rethinking what we mean by perception.

Bergson's 'intuitionism' and James's 'radical empiricism' both dismiss the traditional empiricist notion that external things simply impose themselves on receptive brains. In this much they resist Locke and the Lockean tradition who argue that 'external material things' are the 'objects of SENSATION,' and that the human mind is 'fitted to receive the impressions made on it' in a process that is 'merely passive' (Locke, 1959: 124, 142). For both Bergson and James, the world is dynamic and continuous, not static and discrete; as Bergson says, it is 'unceasing creation, the uninterrupted up-surge of novelty' (Bergson, 1968: 17). For both, perception is at once active and passive, and requires the would-be perceiver to get rightly oriented in and toward the world. Perceiving or intuiting as knowledge by acquaintance is more than sheer mechanical receptivity. Thus, for Bergson, 'philosophy consists in placing oneself within the object itself by an effort of intuition' (Bergson, 1999: 40). Let us turn, then, to a consideration of what James and Bergson have in mind by perception, and as we do so keep in mind the reading of water as an exemplary perceptive act. As we look forward to the last section, it is in being good perceivers that surfers and paddlers are, in some ways at least, potentially good philosophers of a Bergsonian sort.

Perceiving, intuiting, reading

Knowing the world conceptually is an essential human activity and in providing articulate accounts of our experiences lays the groundwork for all human communication. James and Bergson agree that conceptual knowing is analytic and breaks a continuous process into manageable, discrete entities. This way of knowing or understanding the world is, to say the least, extremely useful for getting along in the human world. James indeed believes that 'direct acquaintance and conceptual knowledge' complement each other: 'each remedies the other's defects' (James, 1996: 251). Nevertheless, for both James and Bergson, conceptual or reflective knowing is inadequate on its own for fully knowing reality. It misses what James calls the thickness of experience. Conceiving must give way to perceiving or intuiting. As James argues, 'theoretic knowledge, which is knowledge *about* things, as distinguished from living or sympathetic acquaintance with them, touches only the outer surfaces of reality' (ibid.: 249–50). This inadequacy of 'knowledge about' to the arts of extreme surfing and paddling is something the athletes know well. Perceiving, Bergson's intuiting, is an act of immersion not reflection: 'Dive back into the flux itself, then Bergson tells us, if you wish to know reality rightly' (ibid.: 252). For the soul surfer, says old-school surfer Dick Brewer, it is 'becoming totally involved with the wave and forgetting the outside world' (Brewer, 1997: 4). Obviously, knowledge of this act of perceiving or intuiting must itself be experienced, not merely reflected upon, to be fully known. In Kantian terms, apperception is itself perceptual. Thus, both Bergson and James, rather than schematizing their epistemological accounts, employ description and point to exemplary cases. For James, 'the only way in which to apprehend reality's thickness is either to experience directly by being a part of reality oneself, or to evoke it in imagination by sympathetically divining someone else's inner life' (James, 1996: 250–1).

This intuition of the flux is neither a matter of dominating matter, nor of being dominated by it. Rather, there exists a continuity between agent and world in which intuiting involves mutual influencing. On the one hand, in contrast to the story told by James's intellectualist adversaries, the perceiver does not dictate the order of things from the perspective of a transcendental ego. Intuition is in part 'a kind of passive and receptive listening' (James, 1996: 252–3). Such receptivity is distinct from that of traditional empiricism, however, just insofar as the reception bears dynamic meaning and is not just a collage of inert sense data. On this passive side, we might say that the perceiver in a way *becomes* his object. Intuition is an 'immediate consciousness, a vision which is scarcely distinguishable from the object seen, a knowledge which is contact and even coincidence' (ibid.: 35–6). On this score, it is easy to see the exemplary nature of extreme surfing and paddling. To read effectively the water of a wave or rapid, the athlete must immerse herself in the water itself – in the dynamic situation – either imaginatively or actually. The former may be a rehearsal for the latter. As Ben Solomon suggests, a paddler becomes 'perfectly absorbed in the instant' (Solomon, 1999: 43) and, when reading well, is attentive to the current, to the surface looks that reveal rocks, eddies, and holes, and to the constant changes in the water itself. Insofar as reality is what Bergson calls 'tendency' or 'incipient change of direction,' reflective or conceptual knowing which treats this reality as static would be disastrous in making a run through any extreme rapid (Bergson, 1999: 50). The same receptivity and absorption of the experiencer is a key feature of soul surfing, especially on extreme waves:

> the wave is something you try to flow with, rather than something on which you try to stamp your personality, it's about style, it's a dance . . . it's about not fighting the wave, it's about letting the wave ride you.
>
> (Weaver, 2002: 2)

At the same time, however, the perceiver is active; he is a creator of knowing. The attentiveness is active and demanding and is not in any fundamental way passive – in Emersonian terms, the perceiver is actively receptive: 'We . . . open our senses, clear away as we can all obstruction from the fact, and suffer the intellect to see' (Emerson, 1940: 294). In reading water, for example, a surfer or paddler engages the world in ways that open and close future possibilities in the instant. 'You've got this mountain of water,' says de Villiers, 'and it's changing shape all the time, so your course is never clear . . . When you're riding the wave, you still have some degree of control' (ibid.). The 'reading' is transitorily interpretive and creative as is the emerging, mobile world itself. 'Let us say, then,' Bergson states, 'that in duration, considered as creative evolution, there is a perpetual creation of possibilities and not only of reality' (Bergson, 1999: 21). The paddler or surfer, as perceiver of the water both discovers and creates possibilities in her transactional immersion in the water. Reflectively considered, the surfer or paddler who is immersed in the experience of the moving water acts 'knowingly' in ways that are determinative of what else might occur over the course of the rest of the run. The excellent surfer spontaneously creates her ride as she moves across the face of the wave – this is the freedom Kahanamoku alluded to. The athlete actively places herself 'at the point of view of the thing's interior *doing*' (James, 1996: 262), and, as Candy Calhoun describes, 'through sensitive timing and manoeuvring, the body surfer achieves the beautiful effortlessness of movement that means he is one with the water' (Calhoun, 1966: 168).

What is interesting in both Bergson's and James's notions of knowing through immersion, and what is well exemplified in surfing and paddling, is that knowing is never merely disinterested but is always an ongoing experiment. The 'truth' of one's reading of the water, for example, is to be found in its adeptness for success or failure. In short, knowing and doing are always intimately connected. As Bergson puts it, 'Reality flows; we flow with it; and we call true any affirmation which in guiding us through moving reality, gives us a grip upon it and places us under more favourable conditions for acting' (Bergson, 1999: 255). We see then that through experiences of perceiving or intuiting we become 'experienced' knowers; we are 'trained' by our experience, not by reflection alone, to the point where we become even better perceivers. As Solomon suggests: 'Once you've been trained, you'll understand how the river works' (Solomon, 1999: 36). Thus, a good surfer or paddler *must* be a good perceiver, because the success in being 'one with the water' over time requires an intimate acquaintance. Any human activity, for James and Bergson, should be approachable in this way. What makes extreme paddling and surfing exemplary is the immediate risk and necessary engagement with a phenomenon of nature. They force one to focus on the experience, to engage in intuition, and, in Bergson's terms, to overthrow one's tamer and more superficial conceptual approach to the world. The very risk of failure sharpens the experienced perceiver's ability to read the water. Indeed, one reason to seek bigger waves and steeper rapids is that they hold more promise for yielding a strong sense of knowing. Three-time World Cup whitewater slalom kayak champion Scott Shipley recalls how he and his training companions would paddle the flooded Chilliwack River in winter while others sought flat water. Some days they would paddle a tidal riff in the Skookumchuck Narrows near Vancouver with a wave 35 feet across and 8–10 feet deep in their 20 pound slalom boats: 'This was slalom training at its best' (Shipley, 2001: 16).

Viewed in this way, extreme paddlers and surfers are not mere adrenaline junkies, though they may be that as well. They are, in an aboriginal way, philosophers and metaphysicians; they are, at least, incipient metaphysicians. As highly experienced and trained readers of water, they have an intimate knowing of the world that is accessible only to a few – they understand Bergson's claim that reality *is* flux and change. They have the perceptual skill James believed philosophers should seek: 'a living understanding of the movement of reality' (James, 1996: 264). As a result they are intimately acquainted with the 'thickness' of experience. This in itself should at least in part redeem the extreme athlete from the charge of craziness or loss of senses. But if James and Bergson are right, there are consequences to be had by way of intuition that lie beyond successful runs and adept reading of water. Such perceiving, when experienced, can yield a heightened sense of meaning for the perceiver. In these cases, we would say not only that the athlete has not 'lost her senses' but has, as Thoreau put it, 'come to her senses.'

Perceiving the spiritual

It is interesting that this soulful enhancement of life is widely experienced as a feature of extreme sports but is routinely downplayed as potential hocus pocus in our scientistic age. In *Kayaking on the Edge*, Solomon apologetically introduces a quotation from a teacher of Vipassana meditation that he believes captures something of his experience. On the one hand, he thinks that his readers will 'be struck by the way in which they [the words of the quotation] so accurately describe certain kayaking moments' (Solomon, 1999: 44). The passage focuses on the experience of being 'alive and awake in the here and now' (ibid.). On the other hand, Solomon is almost ashamed to introduce such spiritual language to talk about extreme paddling: he doesn't 'want to dwell on this too much' (ibid.) because it seems out of step in a culture that believes understanding and knowing are to be found only in conceptual accounts of the world, not in feeling alive in the here and now. The very idea of immediate insight seems foreign to scientistic minds, even when scientific theorists throughout Western history often point to something like this in their own experiences. Poincaré and Einstein come to mind, for example. If one goes a step further and suggests that this feeling of awakening and heightened aliveness has a spiritual dimension, one risks ridicule. Yet, as Solomon notes, 'oneness with water' is a very common experience among extreme paddlers. And for some this common experience transforms their attitudes toward and outlooks on life.

What both James and Bergson want to do is to take the mystery and magic out of these intuitive experiences. They do so not by scientizing them or reducing them to psychological mechanisms but by showing that the phenomenon is a very natural one. It is not *ordinary* because it requires the taking of risks and the willingness to overcome the comfort of our Chautauqua-like conceptual worlds in which we believe there is no real contingency. It is extraordinary because few achieve it; it requires the reversal of outlook we noted earlier. But in being extraordinary it is nevertheless an entirely natural human phenomenon, one that can be pointed to not only in music and religion but in the very practices of extreme surfing and paddling with which we are dealing. These perceivers show us what is possible and serve as exemplars for us, even if we only employ such perceiving in much less risky environments, such as a concert hall. When we attentively perceive or intuit our world, we gain an enhanced knowing, and this entails that we enter into meaning – our own spirit and meaning as well as the meanings that emerge in our transactions with the world.

The surfer and the water enter together into the process of reading. Just as with the water, 'we know,' James says, 'the inner movements of our spirit only percep-tually' (James, 1996: 248). If the word 'spirit' is too off-putting, then we simply need to think in terms of 'meaning.' Kahanamoku's famed 'ride' of a mile and a third *meant* something to him and to those who witnessed it. The experience of the ride yielded insight into human existence for Kahanamoku and, vicariously at least, for other surfers who sympathetically entered into this ride by virtue of their own analogous experiences. Again, the bottom line is that numerous extreme athletes achieve this heightened meaning of life when engaged in their practices. It is not a completely esoteric art; it is a human possibility that is exemplified in and through their efforts. As Bergson said, in describing James's outlook on the pervasiveness of this sort of 'religious' experience: 'we bathe in an atmosphere traversed by great spiritual currents' but 'many of us resist, others allow themselves to be carried along' (Bergson, 1999: 252). Surfers and kayakers are among those who allow themselves to be 'carried along.' 'You get inside this wave,' says Tony Weaver, 'inside the stomach of the wave, and you're riding along at the point where that energy changes from one form to another, you get completely filled with some kind of cosmic energy' (Weaver, 2002: 5).

Generating human meaning and enhancing one's learning of reality are philosophical activities. The idealists of the nineteenth century had argued long and hard that only those who had a knack for speculative reasoning could be true philosophers. James and Bergson are more democratically minded and focus on the amateur status of philosophy. Though engaging the world intuitively requires a full reorientation of the intellect, it is a possibility for most humans. We are by nature perceiving beings. Thus we are, most of us, potential philosophers. As Bergson says, 'the act of philosophizing is an easy one' (Bergson, 1999: 149). In looking at extreme surfers and paddlers, then, we might consider them exem-plary amateur philosophers insofar as reading water is thoroughly intuitive – it grasps mobile reality, finds meaning in the world, and creates its own meaning in running the river or riding the wave. Not only do James and Bergson make sense of surfing and paddling perceptual experiences, they provide a backdrop against which all extreme athletes may unapologetically consider the meaning or spiritual dimensions of their practices. In return, extreme surfers and paddlers exemplify the kind of risk and abandonment James and Bergson believe is requisite for the practice of philosophy. They give the rest of us a glimpse of how we might better *see* and *read* the world around us.

Note

1 James, beginning with his *Psychology* routinely talked of experience in terms of flux, flow, and stream.

References

Bergson, H. (1999) *An Introduction to Metaphysics*, trans. T. E. Hulme, Indianapolis, IN: Hackett Publishing Co.

Bergson, H. (1959) *Matter and Memory*, trans. Paul and Palmer, Garden City, NY: Doubleday Anchor Books.

Bergson, H. (1968) *Creative Mind*, New York: Greenwood Press.

Brewer, D. (1997) 'Soul Surfing Interviews', Steve Emery, interviewer, available online at http//www.soulsurfing.com (accessed 31 October 2006), p. 4.

Calhoun, C. (1966) 'Body Surfing', in P. Dixon (ed.) *Men and Waves: A Treasury of Surfing*, New York: Coward-McCann Inc.

Emerson, R. W. (1940) *The Complete Essays and Other Writings of Ralph Waldo Emerson*, ed. B. Atkinson, New York: The Modern Library.

James, W. (1910) *Talks to Teachers on Psychology: And to Students on Some of Life's Ideals*, New York: Henry Holt and Co.

James, W. (1919) *Some Problems of Philosophy*, New York: Longmans, Green, and Co.

James, W. (1996) *A Pluralistic Universe*, Lincoln: University of Nebraska Press.

Kahanamoku, D. (1968) *World of Surfing*, New York: Grosset and Dunlap.

Locke, J. (1959) *An Essay Concerning Human Understanding*, vol. I, New York: Dover Publications.

Shipley, S. (2001) *Every Crushing Stroke*, Atlanta, GA: Crab Apple Publishing.

Solomon, B. (1999) *Kayaking on the Edge*, Birmingham, AL: Menasha Ridge Press.

Ventimiglia, M. (2006) 'Learning and Teaching: Gambling, Love, and Growth', in D. Anderson (ed.) *Philosophy Americana*, New York: Fordham University Press.

Weaver, T. (2002) 'Thrust and Parry', available online at http//www.wavescape.co.za (accessed 31 October 2006).

7   Nature and risk in adventure sports

Kevin Krein

Introduction

One of the characteristic features of adventure sports is the level and type of risk encountered when participating in them. It is not so much the frequency of injuries that is most noticeable, but the possibility of very serious injury, or even death. Moreover, because of the nature of adventure sports, the remoteness of the settings in which they typically take place, and the factors that are beyond the control of participants, such as weather and rockfall in mountaineering, it is impossible to remove such risks from the activities. One simply cannot climb big mountains, surf big waves, or ski steep terrain without exposing oneself to the potential of serious injury or even death.[1] This has led to the view among many commentators, and some athletes, that putting oneself at risk is *the* point of such activities: that athletes participating in such sports do so because they are, among other things, seeking risk. After all, why would anyone put him or herself in such a position when there are so many other less hazardous options for sport and recreation?

I refer to the claim that risk is *the* point of adventure sport as 'risk explanation' since it purports to explain participation in adventure sports by citing the risk involved in those sports. This position, against which I argue, is expressed implicitly or explicitly in almost all discussions of adventure sports in the popular press. In many articles, adventure sports athletes are described as 'thrill junkies,' or as 'hellbent on thrills,' and their motivations are often described as being based in the pursuit of risk.[2]

Here, I argue that while risk is inseparable from many adventure sports, risking death or serious injury is not *the* point of participating in them. There are two parts to my argument in favour of this claim. I first argue that the view that people participate in adventure sports in order to put themselves at risk is problematic. Then, I offer what I believe to be a better explanation of the motivations of athletes and the value of participation in adventure sports. My claim is that adventure sports involve a kind of interaction with the natural world that is not found in other sporting activities, and that the experience of such interaction is valuable enough to justify the acceptance of the risks that accompany such activities.

It should be clear that I am not arguing against the idea that risk is an integral part of adventure sports. Nor am I arguing against the claim that adventure sports athletes often pursue activities in which mistakes have very serious consequences. It is almost certainly the case that one could not remove the hazards from such sports without radically altering the nature of the activities. Additionally, success in such sports depends, to a significant degree, on one's being able to manage risks and respond appropriately to them. This is not the same, however, as saying, as does the so-called 'risk explanation,' that risk is the principal point of the activities or that what participants find most attractive about the activities is risk.

Risky conceptual territory

The goal of this work, then, is to provide a viable philosophical explanation of why people participate in adventure sports. When I say that my explanation is philosophical, I intend to distinguish it, in particular, from psychological, biological, and sociological attempts to explain the desire to participate in such sports. Research on the question of why people participate in adventure sports, and which humans do so, has been done in each of these fields, and I will make use of some of the work that has been accomplished. But the type of explanation I am looking for is not likely to found in the study of biological or psychological traits of adventure sports athletes or by the study of sociological trends. Instead, by considering certain aspects of such sports, I will try to show why they are worth pursuing, despite the risks incurred by participation in them, by at least some rational agents.

This, then, is not an account of the motivations of all adventure sports athletes. Different people participate in sports for different reasons. Statements can be made about the goods obtained by people participating in sports that may apply generally, but we should not expect them to apply to all adventure sports participants.

As a final piece of groundwork, it is important to clarify the nature of the sports with which I am concerned by drawing a distinction between the category of activities I refer to as 'adventure sports' and those that are commonly described in North America as 'extreme sports.' The categories of adventure sports and extreme sports overlap, but it is not the case that all extreme sports are adventure sports. I use 'adventure sports' to refer only to sports that take place in powerful natural environments, and involve the possibility of catastrophic accidents leading to the death of participants. The category of extreme sports, on the other hand, includes all of the alternative sports that are seen in ESPN X-games type venues: rock and ice-climbing in artificial settings, slope-style skiing, skateboarding, and so on. Inclusion in this grouping seems to be as much a matter of fashion as of risk level. Most extreme activities are new, or have, until recently, remained on the fringes of the mainstream. While slope-style skiing and skateboarding are incredibly spectacular, the risks they involve are different from those found in activities in which mistakes, or events unpredictable by humans, lead to fatalities, if not often, then with some regularity.

Difficulties with the risk explanation

With these preliminaries in place, I turn to consideration of the risk explanation. The biggest adventure sports news stories center around accidents. Adventure sports often take place in environments in which the disastrous consequences of some types of errors or mishaps are spectacularly obvious. Given the association of risk with adventure sports, we should expect the popularity of the risk explanation. It is easy to move from the claim that risk and adventure sports are inseparable from the position that the attraction to adventure sports must be based on the risks associated with them.

To do so, however, would be a mistake. It does not follow from the fact that risk is a necessary component of adventure sports, that it is the main point of such sports, or that this is the reason why people participate in them. To infer from the claim that a feature is inseparable from an activity, that that feature is the point of the activity, is to make a logical error. To use William James's often cited example, it does not follow from the fact that every ship crossing the Atlantic burns coal, that burning coal is the purpose of crossing the Atlantic (James, 1890: 558). To use a more current example, though having unprotected sex with numerous partners is a risky activity, it does not follow from this that risk is the point of the activity, or that people who engage in that activity are seeking risk. Claims that the principle point of adventure sports is to experience risk must be supported by a different kind of argument.

One way to approach the issue then, is to ask what role risk plays in the rewards that participants in such sports are expecting to gain. If it is the case that the rewards that attract people to adventure sports are directly produced by the presence of risk, then it seems that risk might be the point of the activities. If not, the risk explanation is unlikely to account for the popularity of adventure sports.

To clarify the risk explanation further, the claim is that adventure sports athletes are attracted by the risk involved in the activities, or the rewards that are a direct result of the risks involved. This excludes from consideration rewards relating to public recognition or monetary gain for doing exceptionally risky things. If Evel Knievel is willing to risk his life attempting to jump the Snake River Canyon because he thinks doing so will make him rich and famous, the risk explanation, as I have outlined it, will not account for his behavior. Presumably, if he felt that he could gain fortune and fame some other way, and avoid the risks involved in a death-defying leap, he would do so. On the other hand, if he jumps the canyon because he wants to experience the feeling of risking his life, or something directly related to the risk he is taking, such as the feeling of self-satisfaction that comes specifically from performing well in a risky situation rather than in any other, the attraction of the situation is the presence of the risk involved.

Another way of putting this is to say that the risk explanation requires that the principal value of adventure sports is intrinsic to the activities and stems from the risks involved in them. Here, I follow Mike McNamee's use of 'intrinsic value' which refers to 'those subjective psychological satisfactions which are the direct benefits of an activity and which flow from the internal goods associated with the activity' (McNamee 1994: 305). The risk explanation then, will not account for the value of adventure sports if either the principal value of the activities is intrinsic and stems from some feature or combination of features other than risk, or if the value of the activities is merely instrumental. In such a case the link between the external good and risk is not strong enough to warrant the claim that the risk is the reason for participation in the activity.

Considering the motivations of adventure sports athletes is simplified by the fact that the rewards of honor and money gained in such activities are rarely significant enough to explain the sacrifices such athletes make in pursuit of their sports. External rewards of this sort simply cannot justify the effort and expense devoted to such activities. Consider the ratio of effort to likely external rewards in backcountry skiing and climbing. Both are sports that require years of work to acquire the skills and knowledge needed to attain even a small amount of recognition or monetary reward, let alone glory. Such sports certainly have their stars, but the external rewards pale in comparison to sports that have larger spectator and participant bases. In North America, while the names of football and basketball heroes are known in nearly every household, the best climbers and free skiers are virtually unknown. While these sports go through periods of popularity with the press, there is little glory for the athletes therein.

One might protest that the recent boom in extreme sports competition and marketing are counter-examples to this claim. It is important to note, however, that many of the most successful athletes in such sports acquired their skills during a time in which the activities received little media attention. Brett Downs captures this point in his essay, 'Small Bikes, Big Men,' while describing the sudden popularity of BMX riding:

> All of a sudden my sport became 'extreme' and the public became aware of what I have been doing all these years. This media exposure is what enables me to write this chapter, yet it has nothing to do with why I ride or my values.
>
> (Downs, 2003: 145)

Furthermore, the sports that have benefited the most from the recent X-boom are those that can be easily placed in a constructed, controlled, and transportable environment; the X-Games need to occur in a place that is convenient for spectators to attend. In such environments, the risk of catastrophic accidents is greatly reduced. This means that the type of adventure sports with which I am concerned here are generally excluded from such events. While perceived risk draws crowds, competitors do not die at the X-games – death is bad news for the sponsors who simply will not tolerate its possibility. Thus, while skateboarding and BMX have benefited greatly from the X-boom, mountaineering, big mountain free skiing, and big wave surfing have gained far less.

If there are rewards, then they must be of a more internal kind, such as pleasure, exhilaration or self-satisfaction. One can certainly obtain such internal rewards in adventure sports settings. But, again, we need to stick to the question of whether risk is the primary point of such activities, or the primary cause of the rewards. The question is whether these are direct products of risk, or, instead, of other aspects of the activities. As in the case of external rewards, in adventure sports, the ratio of time spent to internal rewards directly dependent on risk is great. Further, there are much easier ways to experience risk available to just about any human being. Consider skiing, climbing, and surfing. Developing the skills to participate in such sports requires significant time and effort, yet people devote themselves to such activities. If it were primarily risk that participants were after, there are certainly easier and more convenient ways to find it. One can drive fast (leaving the seatbelt unbuckled is one way to increase the risk even more) or just engage in a game of Russian roulette. If adrenaline rushes associated with danger are what one is after, there are plenty of activities more convenient than adventure sports.

Furthermore, any cursory study of adventure sports athletes will show that most put extensive effort into taking precautions to limit the risks of their activities rather than attempt to increase them. It is easy enough to make otherwise safe environments hazardous. Adventure sports athletes spend much of their time involved in the far more difficult task of reducing the risks found in extremely hazardous environments by using equipment or by developing their knowledge and skills.

So far, I have offered three lines of argument against the claim that people pursue adventure sports because they are risky: I argued first that the mere association of risk and adventure sports is not sufficient to show that risk is the point of the activities; second, I argued that, if one exposes oneself to risk for the sake of external rewards, then the point of the activity is the reward rather than the risk itself; and finally, I argued that, in the case of internal rewards, which could be the direct result of experiencing risk, because adventure sports require significant effort and often sacrifice on the part of athletes, it does not seem that risk itself could be the point of those activities. To this line of argument I added two observations: first, that there are much easier ways to put oneself at risk than participation in adventure sports; and second, that adventure athletes often attempt to limit the amount of risk involved in their sports. These arguments and observations cast serious doubt on the risk explanation.

Tempting fate: the death instinct

Still, there is one view that is presented often enough to deserve special attention. This stems from the theoretical claim that tempting death is the result of some kind of innate drive and that it satisfies an inner need. It certainly seems to be the view on which the popular media's explanation of the growth of adventure sports is based. For example, the *Time* magazine cover story mentioned above claims that, while our lives are relatively risk-free, humans used to face risks on a regular basis, then suggests that we may still have a psychological need to seek risky situations:

traditional risks have been reduced by science, government or legions of personal injury lawyers, leaving boomers and Generations X and Y to face less real risk. Life expectancy has increased. You are 57% less likely to die of heart disease than your parents; smallpox, measles and polio have virtually been eradicated.

Combat survivors speak of the terror and excitements of playing in a death match. Are we somehow incomplete as people if we do not taste that terror and excitement on the brink?

(Greenfield, 1999: 32)

On the face of it, the claim that humans, or at least some of us, have an inner desire to risk death is a bit odd. Nevertheless, it does have a history of serious consideration. The most influential source to which this belief can be traced is Freud's positing of the death instinct in *The Ego and the Id*. Freud argued that all human desires stem from one of two sources originating in that most primitive part of the self, the id. The first of these is generally referred to as the life instinct and includes the desire to procreate and to preserve oneself. The second of these is the death instinct, 'the task of which is to lead organic life back into the inanimate state' (Freud, [1923] 1960: 38). According to Freud, these instincts beget base desires, such as the desire to procreate as much as possible in the case of the life instinct, and the desire to commit suicide in the case of the death instinct. If left unchecked, these desires would lead to socially unacceptable and self-destructive behaviors. Fortuitously, Freud argues, the ego, when healthy, redirects these desires so that they lead to acceptable behaviors that can, indirectly, satisfy the instinctual drives. Regrettably, however, the ego is not always successful at redirecting base instincts toward optimally beneficial behaviors. In some individuals with less healthy egos, the death instinct leads to actually flirting with death, or teasing it, by taking risks. This theory has worked its way deeply into popular culture, and provides the basis for the most commonly accepted explanation of the popularity of adventure sports – that enthusiasts participate in them because they are driven to do so by an inner need to risk their own lives.

While using the death instinct as an explanation of the participation in adventure sports is extremely popular, there are very good reasons to doubt its viability. The most decisive of these comes from more recent developments in psychological research. In the 1970s, Marvin Zuckerman created what he termed the 'sensation seeking scale' as a way of measuring what he refers to as the sensation seeking personality trait. The trait is defined by 'the seeking of varied, novel, complex, and intense, sensations and experiences, and the willingness to take physical, social, legal, and financial risks for the sake of such experiences' (Zuckerman, 1994: 27). One's sensation seeking score is determined by a questionnaire which asks whether one likes to try new foods, go to wild parties, meet new people, etc. A large body of research supports the claim that the scale is impressively predictive of a number of types of behavior.[3] It turns out, as one might guess, that people who participate in adventure sports tend to score high on sensation seeking tests.[4]

The question of whether sensation seekers in general pursue risk for its own sake, is relevant to the question addressed in this chapter concerning risk and the motivations of people who choose to participate in adventure sports. Sensation seekers do take more risks than others, but, as I argued above, it does not follow from this fact that risk is the attraction of such sports. Zuckerman explicitly makes this point, maintaining that:

> few sensation seekers, outside of the antisocial ones, seek to maximize risk for its own sake. Most accept the risk and attempt to minimize it. The low sensation seekers are not just risk aversive; they see no point or reward in the sensation-seeking activities that could justify what they regard as the high levels of risk involved.
>
> (Zuckerman, 1994: 27)

This claim is supported by studies showing, for instance, that while sensation seekers are more likely than others to break speed laws while driving, male sensation seekers who speed are just as likely as anyone else to wear seatbelts. Moreover, while high sensation seekers tend to engage in a wide variety of sexual activities and to have a larger lifetime number of sexual partners than low sensation seekers, as a group, they are no less likely than lower sensation seekers to use condoms or other methods of contraception (ibid.: 145).[5]

The argument is that, if sensation seeking behavior were really about the risks involved, then we would expect sensation seekers to attempt to enhance the level of risk in their activities. That they do not means that risk seems not to be the main purpose of sensation seeking behavior.[6] It is because adventure sports are a *specific* type of sensation seeking activity, that the *general* arguments applies to them.

According to Freudian theory and the popular media, some people, or all people to some degree, have an inner need to pursue risk, and, if circumstances do not provide them with risky situations, they create them – hence, the birth of adventure sports. The alternative picture I am presenting is that people are willing, to varying degrees, to tolerate risk in the pursuit of other goals.

The nature of adventure sports

If it is true that participants in adventure sports are not pursuing risk, but rather that they accept it because they value the experiences obtained by participation in such sports, we can then ask what it is about the nature of such activities and the experiences they yield that makes them so attractive. Here, we move from psychology back to philosophy in order to address the issue.

We know that people participate in sports in general. What I will focus on is why people participate in adventure sports rather than mainstream sports. Doing so will help develop an explanation of the differences between adventure and mainstream sports and will lead to a better explanation of what it is about the former that may make participating in them worth the risks.

In addressing the question, one must explicitly draw a distinction that will help clarify the types of risk encountered in adventure sports. 'Risk' is often defined as the potential for losing something of value.[7] It is important, however, to notice a difference between two types of risk encountered by adventure sports enthusiasts. First, there are hazards that are out of the control of participants and must simply be accepted if an athlete is going to participate in a particular activity or pursue a specific objective. For example, climbing some routes requires exposing oneself to the possibility of rock or ice fall from above. In some such instances, there is little one can do to mitigate the risk. Knowledge or skill are not the determining factors in whether or not climbers survive intentional exposure to such risks. On the other hand, there are features of the natural landscape that hurt only those who make mistakes. These are risks that are mitigated by skill and experience. For example, there are slopes that are regularly skied by very good skiers, but which, if attempted by less skilled athletes would very likely result in injury or death. Consider the activity of free soloing rock (intentionally climbing without a rope). Free soloing is, in a sense, a very dangerous activity. There is little room for error since falling almost certainly results in death. Surprisingly, perhaps, very few climbers have died while intentionally free soloing routes. From 1951 to 1984, there were 850 climbing related deaths; only one of those deaths was a free soloist – in fact, the only well-known free soloist to have died while practicing the sport is Derek Hersey, who fell while soloing Yosemite's Sentinel Rock in 1993 (Soden, 2003).

It can be said that that the goal of adventure athletes is not to leave survival up to chance, or to gamble with one's life, but instead that they seek situations in which they have control and responsibility for their lives and in which survival depends on their judgment and skills. Once this distinction is recognized, a different picture of the adventure athlete emerges. Rather than characterizing adventure athletes as reckless thrill seekers (as the risk explanation does) those involved in adventure sports can be seen as athletes attempting to develop their skills so that they can take on more difficult challenges. The mischaracterization of adventure sports in the popular media is, at least in part, a result of failing to recognize this distinction outlined above.

Of course, it cannot be denied that adventure sports athletes do seek out situations in which the consequences of mistakes are very serious. And there is certainly a measure of satisfaction that comes with being directly responsible for one's own safety and an opportunity to assess one's strengths and weaknesses in an environment in which mistakes have very serious consequences. But this does not generally involve flirting with death or putting oneself in situations in which death seems close at hand. When there are close calls, they are the result of uncontrollable hazards, or mistakes that result from an athlete choosing an objective that is not within his or her ability, or from carelessness on the part of the athlete. None of these experiences is pursued directly.

Of course, adventure sportspersons must accept the fact that they cannot always be sure of their own safety. Snow stability, for example, is difficult to assess. When skiing steep slopes, avalanches can be difficult to predict. Practitioners do their best to stay away from unstable terrain, but there is usually some degree of danger that simply must be accepted. It should be clear, however, that skiers and snow-boarders typically do their best to stay away from avalanche danger just as climbers attempt to avoid areas in which rock fall from above is a hazard. These are the hazards that are often accepted in order to achieve some other goal. The question that needs to be answered then is why athletes accept objective hazards that are out of their control. With this in mind, I turn to an explicit consideration of a distinctive feature of adventure sports that makes them worth participating in, in spite of the risks involved.

There is an obvious feature that adventure sports have in common with each other and which differentiates them from mainstream sports. Most sport activity takes place in environments that are standardized, controlled, and generally contain right angles. Sports such as baseball, basketball, and football (American, European, and Australian rules) take place on flat, measured playing fields. Figure skating and diving competitions, as well, take place in standard-sized rinks and pools with platforms of measured height. In races, such as rallying in Formula 1, running, and swimming, all competitors use the same course, or one measured to be very similar. In what are commonly referred to as adventure sports, this is not typically the case. Mountaineering and ice-climbing routes often change significantly from one day to the next and from year to year. One of the ultimate feats in these sports is climbing a route that has not been climbed before and one of the skills of the sport is in knowing under what conditions a particular route is achievable. When surfing, one is in an environment that is changing from moment to moment, and, again, knowledge of the behavior of the ocean is considered part of the sport's demands.

We can combine this observation with the claim that, in adventure sports, some aspect of the natural environment takes over the role that is played by human competitors in traditional sports. This is not a new idea. In 1968, John W. Loy Jr, for example, argued that sports always involve competition. In some cases this is competition against individuals, teams, or oneself, and in some cases it can be 'competition between an individual or a team and an inanimate object of nature, e.g. a canoeist running a set of rapids or a mountain climbing expedition' (Loy, 1968: 5). One traditional way of putting this is to say that in such sports, athletes compete against nature.

There is a difficulty, however, with this description of the situation. Competition generally requires at least two competitors, and claiming that athletes compete against features of the natural world requires that we anthropomorphize those features. It is more correct to say that features of the natural world provide opportunities for tests. In the case of a mountain for example, the test may simply be to reach the summit, or to do so by a particular route, or to do so within a certain time limit.[8]

This way of describing the climber's relationship with the natural world is consistent with the conception of adventure sports in which mountains, rivers, and other features of the natural world are said to be conquered by athletes. A great many contemporary adventure athletes, however, would not accept this type of characterization of the activities in which they are involved. The idea of 'conquering' some aspect of the natural environment has largely been replaced by the idea of interactively harmonizing with it. While participating in an athletic pursuit, this requires adjusting one's actions in response to changes in the environment in an attempt to achieve gracefulness and fit.

Whether one takes adventure athletes to be surmounting, or harmonizing with, the natural environment, it is clear that adventure sports require interacting with the environment in intricate ways. Loy's claim, then, can be replaced with the broader assertion that in adventure sports, rather than interacting with human competitors, participants (either as individuals or teams), one is primarily interacting with some feature of the natural world. At times, it may be that athletes perceive themselves to be attempting to overcome some feature of the natural world. At other times, it may be that a natural feature, such as a wave or a steep slope being skied with snow constantly sloughing off, is more akin to working with a partner in figure skating.

Before moving on, there is a competing characterization of competition, also mentioned by Loy, that is worth considering. This is the idea that in adventure sports one may compete against oneself. This is certainly one way of characterizing what is happening in adventure sports. In activities such as high altitude mountaineering, the ability to push oneself is a tremendous asset. I resist this characterization. First, the same difficulty considered above – that competition requires two active competitors – still pertains. Perhaps even more significantly, there is a distinction between adventure sports, in a constantly changing environment, and sports in which one faces the same, or similar, conditions repeatedly. Consider running races in which one is trying to better one's personal best. Athletes in such situations are always striving to be faster than their previous performances. This makes sense only if the distance one is measuring is constant and the environment in which one runs is sufficiently similar. Without such consistency, 'competing against oneself' is a much less felicitous description of what is occurring. Yet, in a sport such as mountaineering or skiing, while one certainly improves, and is trying to learn from experience and practice, the conditions under which the sport takes place offer no precise measure of improvement. One might say that the athlete aims to outdo his or her prior accomplishments. Nevertheless, particularly if we keep in mind that future accomplishments will be difficult to compare to former ones, saying that an athlete is competing with himself or herself does not felicitously articulate the situation. On the other hand, speaking of interacting with the natural world does capture what is central to these activities.

Interacting with nature through sport

There is more to say, of course, about the character of the interaction between adventure athletes and the natural environment. In a particularly insightful passage, mountain biker Lee Bridger makes the following claim:

> The single most important draw of riding a mountain bike is NATURE – not
> the environmentalist, tree hugging, untouchable nature of Sierra Club twits
> who try to make themselves look like caring people by keeping you off the
> grass so they can buy a three-million-dollar home and have the mountains
> untouched in their picture window – but the nature that you can just dive
> into and have sex with.
>
> (Bridger, 2003: 186)

While I would not endorse her characterization of the Sierra Club, her characterization of what is one of the most attractive features of adventure sports – the
opportunity to have an intensely palpable interactive relationship with nature
– is apposite. One could argue that it is attractive simply because it offers the
opportunity for an intimate connection with nature and that this is something
many human beings desire. While I think that there is truth in this claim, I take
here a different approach. I argue that for those interested in athletic activities,
the interactions between humans and the natural world found in adventure
sports are valuable because of the potential they offer for exceptional athletic
experiences.

What is interesting about Bridger's use of the metaphor of sex is that it is an
activity in which, in its most common instantiation, two partners play active
roles. In successful sexual activity, partners interact with, and react to, each
other. A good game is one that is played between two competitors who bring out
the best in each other, who force each other to react to unpredictable maneuvers,
and who ultimately work together to create a beautiful and dramatic interaction.
Great experiences and achievements in adventure sports occur under analogous
conditions. An adventure sport event is successful when interaction with the
natural world brings out the best in an athlete by providing challenges and
original and interesting situations to which the athlete appropriately reacts.

There are, of course, limitations to the analogy. In traditional sports (as well as
sex), hopefully, both partners are active and aware of each other. In the case of
adventure sports, the relationship is noticeably one-sided. Mountains do not care
whether they are skied or climbed and waves do not change their course for
surfers. In the case of adventure sports, this does not necessarily detract from the
aesthetic value of the experience or the value of the interaction for the athlete.

The forces of nature and the limitations that adventure athletes put on
themselves make it the case that the environment is obviously more powerful
than the athletes. Surfers cannot redirect waves; skiers cannot stop the pull of
gravity; and climbers can do nothing about the duration and severity of the
weather. The only way to succeed in adventure sports situations, then, is to react
appropriately to the environment and the changes presented. While not a
conscious participant, the natural world can take on the role of a partner with
which one must interact. This is true whether or not one experiences that
situation as being one of combat against, or harmonizing with, one's environment. This brings us, finally, to an answer to the question of why adventure sports
are worth pursuing, even if they require putting oneself at risk.

In adventure sports, the other 'participant' in the game might be a 10 meter wave, 800 meter, 60 degree couloir, or an 8,000 meter peak, rather than a human competitor. It is my claim that the opportunity to play with such awesome partners is one of the principal sources of the attraction of adventure sports.[9]

For one who takes sports seriously, the opportunity to take part in sports activities under conditions that make it possible to engage with natural features more powerful than any conceivable human being, is at least worth considering. Most athletes and lovers of sport are interested in sporting events that are likely to produce dramatic and beautiful interactions. It should be clear that adventure sports contexts are pregnant with rich possibilities.

Considering adventure sports from this perspective helps us to explain why this is the case. Athletes are constantly evaluating their abilities and trying to extend them. At the same time, in adventure sports, mistakes can be catastrophic. When playing with such powerful forces, overestimating one's abilities is akin to hubris. Even if one is not challenging the gods, attempting to play games with them can be an equally dangerous prospect. Nevertheless, it can also be a very rewarding one whose attractions are obvious.

What is even clearer is how the risk involved in such sports can be intimately connected with the rewards of the activity, but not be its goal. Interacting with powerful and unpredictable features of the natural world requires fluid responses that challenge human abilities. This is one of the deepest goals of athletic participation. But the features that challenge, and often bring out the best in adventure athletes, also contain dangers.

Conclusion

I began this chapter with the claim that the risk explanation is the most common conception of why people participate in adventure sports. I also pointed out that the popularity of the risk explanation is likely a result of the fact that risk is probably the most readily apparent feature shared by adventure sports. I argued first that the risk explanation does not follow from the obvious presence of risk. Further, I have tried to replace the risk explanation with one that takes into account the difficulties and effort required by participants in adventure sports, as well as the significant time and effort athletes put into attempting to reduce the risk involved in their respective activities. Adventure sports are risky, but risk is best understood as a by-product, rather than the goal, of such sports. The choice to participate in adventure sports can be justified by the relationship with the natural world and the potential for meaningful athletic experience provided by such sports.

Acknowledgments

I would like to thank Stefan Ricci and Abigail Levin for their helpful criticism of, and comments on, earlier drafts of this chapter.

Notes

1 The sports to which I will most often refer are related to climbing and skiing – mountaineering, backcountry skiing and snowboarding, and ski mountaineering – simply because these are the relevant activities with which I am most familiar. However, what I say is generally transferable to all adventure sports.
2 See, for example, McCarthy (2004) and Hamilton and Miller (2004).
3 See Zuckerman (1994) for a comprehensive review of the literature in this area. He reports that between 1979 and 1990 there were over 400 publications in the psychological literature under the term 'sensation seeking.' His 1994 book includes chapters providing an overview of research on the relationship between sensation seeking and sports and vocations, social and sexual relationships, drinking and drug use, etc.
4 On this point, see chapter 6 of Zuckerman (1994). See also, Cronin (1990), and Jack and Ronan (1998).
5 Zuckerman cites Clement and Jonah (1984) who write in support of the former point and White and Johnson (1988) with reference to the latter.
6 One might imagine that a Freudian could respond that if it is the death instinct that motivates such risky behavior, and the sensation seeking behavior does release the tension or energy propelling behind the motivation, then there is no need to increase the danger of one's activities. In this case, one could say that the ego has done its job by directing the instinctual drives of the id into behaviors that do not actually lead to the destruction of the self. But, at this point it becomes unclear whether the theory has any predictive power at all – if any behavior, whether it maximizes or minimizes risk is explained by the theory, then we have to ask in what sense the theory is doing any explanatory work? This seems to be an instance of the general criticism Karl Popper directs toward Freudian theory – if in principle it explains any possible behavior then a theory is unfalsifiable and therefore unscientific. See, for example, Popper (1963: 139–57).
7 See, for example, Priest and Gass (2005: 18).
8 For an in-depth discussion of this point see Kretchmar (1975).
9 It is interesting, given the position for which I am now arguing, how often adventure sports athletes anthropomorphize features in the natural environment or see themselves as being in a relationship that actually is two-sided.

References

Bridger, L. (2003) 'Out of the Gene Pool and Into the Food Chain', in R. Rinehart and S. Sydnor (eds.) *To the Extreme: Alternative Sports, Inside and Out*, Albany, NY: State University of New York Press, 179–89.

Clement, R. and Jonah, B. A. (1984) 'Field Dependence, Sensation Seeking and Driving Behavior', *Personality and Individual Differences*, 5: 87–93.

Cronin, C. (1990) 'Sensation Seeking Among Mountain Climbers', *Personality and Individual Differences*, 12: 653–4.

Downs, B. (2003) 'Small Bikes, Big Men', in R. Rinehart and S. Sydnor (eds.) *To the Extreme: Alternative Sports, Inside and Out*, Albany, NY: State University of New York Press, 145–52.

Freud, S. ([1923]1960), *The Ego and the Id*, trans. J. Riviere, ed. J. Strachey, New York: W.W. Norton & Company.

Greenfield, K. T. (1999) 'Life on the Edge', *Time*, September 6, 154, (10): 29–36.

Hamilton, K. and Miller, S. (2004) 'Outer Limits', *Newsweek*, June 19, 125, (25): 78–82.

Jack, S. J. and Ronan K.R. (1998) 'Sensation Seeking Among High and Low-Risk Sports

Participants', *Personality and Individual Differences*, 25: 1063–83.

James, W. (1890) *Principles of Psychology*, vol. II, New York: Henry Holt.

Kretchmar, R. S. (1975) 'From Test to Contest: An Analysis of Two Kinds of Counterpoint in Sport', *Journal of the Philosophy of Sport*, II: 23–30.

Loy, J. (1968) 'The Nature of Sport: A Definitional Effort', *Quest*, 10: 1–15.

McCarthy, T. (2004) 'When The Surf's Way Up: Who Cares if it's Dangerous?' *Time*, July 19, 164: 64–7.

McNamee, M. J. (1994) 'Valuing Leisure Practices: Towards a Theoretical Framework', *Leisure Studies*, 13(1): 288–309.

Popper, K. (1963) *Conjectures and Refutations: The Growth of Scientific Knowledge*, London: Routledge and Kegan Paul.

Priest, S. and Gass, M. (2005) *Effective Leadership in Adventure Programming*, Champaign, IL: Human Kinetics.

Soden, G. (2003) *Falling: How Our Greatest Fear Became Our Greatest Thill – A History*, New York: W.W. Norton and Company.

White, H. R. and Johnson, V. (1988) 'Risk Taking as a Predictor of Adolescent Sexual Activity and Use of Contraception', *Journal of Addiction Research*, 3: 317–31.

Zuckerman, M. (1994) *Behavioral Expressions and Biosocial Bases of Sensation Seeking*, New York: Cambridge University Press.

8 Aesthetic and ethical issues concerning sport in wilder places[1]

Alan P. Dougherty

Introduction

During the second half of the twentieth century there was an exponential growth of participation in adventurous sports undertaken in relatively wild locations.[2] This was especially true amongst the populations of economically favoured countries, and this trend appears to continue unabated into the new millennium.[3] Indeed, to the extent that members of such populations engage with wilder places at all recreation is the context in which this typically happens. This chapter follows an optimistic line of argument. It proposes that when sporting engagement with wilder places is both authentic and appropriate, the quality of sporting experience is both likely to be greater and that negative environmental impacts will be reduced. Although the chapter is partly a consideration of how humans relate properly to some of the wilder places that the planet still retains, it is principally an exploration of the contention that by following an ethic of appropriate and authentic engagement in practice, human sporting experience of wilder places will also be enhanced. It should be acknowledged from the outset that this line of argument is underpinned by a strong presupposition that the wilder places of the Earth have both intrinsic qualities, and instrumental value to humans, which warrant both recognition and value in the context of respect-ful engagement. A further and important basis of this chapter is the contention that the human species is inextricably part of environment[4] but that it is a sub-set apparently unique in its potential for both large-scale influence and, crucially to the central arguments of this chapter, the ability to engage in ethically guided practice.

Why 'wilder place' not wilderness?

Central to the discussion of the argument pertaining to appropriate and authentic engagement of the kind proposed is the concept of a 'wilder place'. The concept is relational. It is applicable to locations that are relatively natural, which is to say, relatively free from human influence. The concept has been adopted in preference to the concept of 'wilderness' for a variety of reasons:

1   The debate over wilderness is becoming increasingly sterile (indeed, almost pointless) because it is unlikely that anywhere on the planet can be shown to

be entirely free from human influence (at least if one accepts 'non-deliberate' influences such as pollution).

2   It seems clearer to offer an alternative nomenclature for a newly defined concept rather than retain 'wilderness' and redefine its conceptual basis.

3   Wilderness tends to be used as an absolute concept: either a location is or is not depicted as 'wilderness'. This is not helpful. Although mutually exclusive notions of the natural and the humanised are useful as tools for contrast and comparison, reality presents us with a variety of wild locations. Whatever term is applied, its conceptual basis needs to be applicable to that variety of locations, the ecosystems of which demonstrate differing degrees of naturalness and extent of human influence. Additionally, if wilderness is used as an absolute concept then there is a tendency to suggest that it only has intrinsic value or is of anthropocentric good if in pristine condition. It can be argued, however, that a variety of wilder places (which could not be described as wilderness when the term is used in an absolute sense) hold both intrinsic value and potentiality for instrumental value as places where human good may be found. Adopting the idea of 'wilder places' allows for a gradation of wilder experiences. It allows consideration of environments of varying wildness or with varying potential for wildness of experience.

4   Wilderness has become an increasingly contentious concept.[5] It is a term almost guaranteed to raise hackles whenever it is applied. There is a tendency for discussions of proper human engagement with more natural environments to be subjugated by the increasingly moribund debate over the definition of wilderness. For example, the classic wilderness debate in North America stems significantly from the misapplication of the term by, mainly European, settlers as they moved westwards propelled (apparently) by a Christian zeal to make good *use* of hitherto *unproductive* land. Such misapplication took no note of the fact that the land they were traversing was already home to Native Americans. Archaeological and historical evidence has demonstrated increasingly that the indigenous populations had deliberately altered their environment by thinning scrub to facilitate hunting or in the cultivation of crops.[6] The nomadic lifestyle of some Native Americans, later to be popularised by cinema, only became especially viable after the introduction of the horse by the Spanish. By contrast, in the UK one is dealing almost exclusively with landscapes that have been humanised to varying degrees. This fact has been influential in the rise to prominence of the notion of the cultural landscape,[7] albeit with, often, too little regard for the environmental constraints under which such landscapes became humanised. The use of the term wilderness is very likely to annoy the upland farming community in their rather self-righteous role as 'creators' of landscapes. In the Scottish Highland context, increasing historical sensibility and the rise of Gaelic politics has drawn upon evidence of a humanised landscape prior to the forced depopulation of the Clearances,[8] and thus the application of the term wilderness, even to areas which have been humanised only marginally, becomes problematic.

The adoption of the term 'wilder place' has the potential to be less contentious so that debate can actually move forward to real issues of contemporary importance.

Authentic engagement, wilder places and wilder experiences

It is sometimes suggested that the seas are the last great wilderness around the UK. In terms of a definition of wilderness as free from human influence this is, of course, incorrect. What the seas can offer, however, is an authentically wilder experience.

It is important to distinguish between a wilder place and wilder experience. The latter can take place in a partly humanised landscape. For example, during bad weather, mountaineering in the Cairngorms can offer an authenticity of engagement with a wilder place – a truly wilder experience with potentially fatal consequences. Yet, although this big country in the Scottish context and subject to weather of Antarctic ferocity, this area of mountains could not correctly be termed wilderness in an absolute sense.

An authentically wilder experience can even take place in the surreal setting of a major trunk road. An occasion comes to mind of taking part, as a member of a local mountain rescue team, in the recovery of motorists stranded in a severe blizzard. The experience was truly a wilder one in the sense that an accident or poor judgement could have had just as serious consequences if the location had been somewhere classically wilder. The engagement with environment, especially in respect of the atmospheric and under-foot conditions, was authentically wilder, despite the humanised location.

Appropriate and authentic engagement with specific environments ought to be considered as guiding principles of interaction. Guided by Nature, such a model should engender behaviour appropriate to the well-being of the ecology and wildness of an area and, it will be argued, encourage and facilitate an enhanced sporting experience. Appropriate engagement should be sought because it is ethically and aesthetically sound with respect to location, while authenticity of engagement is to be found in that relationship to environment which is not overly mediated by technology. Under this description, practice would be guided by the principle of *adapting the activity to the environment*, rather than the environment to the activity.

Authenticity in engagement with wilder places

The concept of authentic engagement is not offered as an absolutist idea. In practice most, if not all, of our relation to environment is mediated to some extent by technology; indeed one definition of a human being is as a tool-using animal. In the context of sport in wilder places, an important distinction needs to be made between the concepts of authenticity *of self* and of authenticity *of process*.

The idea of the authentic self, from which I wish to distinguish my specific use of authenticity of process, can be traced back, for example, via Rousseau and

Augustine to Socrates. Only latterly did it become a key concept for the Existentialists. Kierkegaard distinguished between a personally chosen authentic self and a public identity. Nietzsche made a similar distinction. Influenced by both Kierkegaard and Nietzsche, Heidegger also distinguished between a resolutely recognised authentic individuality and one's public identity. In turn, Sartre's subsequent notions of good faith and bad faith are largely concerned with adherence, or otherwise, to an internalised concept of authenticity. The concept of authenticity of self has, however, been criticised both for a lack of clarity in its presentation and as an impossible ideal.

Heidegger's *one's own essential being-in-the-world*, with its relative lack of a mind/environment dualism, begins to broaden the conceptual scope of authenticity. It opens up the possibility that authenticity can be fruitfully conceptualised as a process when we engage ourselves with the environment. This contrasts with the previously mentioned notions of the authentic self, which rest largely upon a concept of mind as dislocated in some way from environment.

Guignon (2004) offers a compelling critique of the essentially inward-looking accounts of authenticity which were hitherto central to the philosophical discussions in the Western tradition. His alternative emphasis upon authenticity as a concept of *relational engagement* with other persons can be extended and developed to consider authenticity as a concept concerning the nature of our interface with environment. Influenced by this posture, the remainder of the chapter is an attempt to apply such a concept of authenticity: as a relational engagement in the context of the interface between environment and humans engaged in sporting activity.

By meeting Nature more on its own terms, authentic engagement can become a defining characteristic of behaviour towards the sentient and non-sentient elements of wilder places. Guided by Nature, despite the dynamics of ecosystems but because of their potential to endure, the concept should not be prone to criticisms of ephemerality. Allowing an ethical and aesthetic respect for Nature to be its central principles, this characteristic not only has the potential to respond to varying degrees of past and present human interaction with locations but, moreover, to guide current and future engagement with wilder places. Authenticity becomes both a necessary condition for appropriate engagement with wilder places and a precondition to enhanced sporting experience when engaging in such a context.

A helpful contrast can be made between authentic and inauthentic engagement in the sense of that one is either guided by environment's own terms or one is not. Consider the example, of oxygen-reliant, guided ascents of Everest, arranged commercially that, as Simpson (1997: 60) puts it, '[do] tend to pander to the egotistic ambitions of individuals who otherwise wouldn't dream of attempting such an ascent'. Once it had been recognised that exceptional and well-acclimatised mountaineers can operate at 8,000 metres plus, practice guided by authenticity would suggest that those of lesser ability, unable to meet this term of Nature, should engage with a project more suited to their ability.[9] By doing so the appalling levels of litter on the mountain (much of it discarded oxygen tanks) would be lessened and the quality of the mountaineering experience much enhanced by the reduction in numbers. Likewise, in the less rarefied context of British mountaineering, *the long walk in principle*[10] is also self-selecting. Its application limits access on the basis of ability and effort, and that is surely ethically much more sound than, say, on a charging basis. It too reduces environmental impact and enhances human experience.

No doubt such examples will be countered by claims of elitism. The approach is elitist but in a *non-pejorative* sense. It recognises that all individuals will be limited by their physical and mental abilities, not least of all by their carrying capacity, and that these are likely to vary over time. One must bear in mind the limited ability of a habitat to cope with particular levels of demand. For example, an area of grazing land will only be able to sustain without detriment a certain herd size. In the context of recreation, carrying capacity might be seen to have been exceeded when, for example, serious footpath erosion takes place. Such exceeding of carrying capacity might be alleviated by management, such as path repair or construction, but could ultimately result in an unsustainable situation. This is especially true when the number of people visiting an area in search of relative solitude becomes so high that the isolation sought becomes impossible. Ignoring the broader notion of carrying capacity can result in both environmental damage and reduced adventurous sporting experience. Adherence to some notion of carrying capacity and the restriction of access according to self-selection on the basis of ability and willingness to self-reliance tends to result in a more authentic engagement with environment.

Authentic engagement with environment contrasts with the life experience of many in the Developed World: disengagement from environment; *Disneyfication* and its sanitised presentation of Nature; and the vicarious pleasures of virtual reality. The routine of home, car, indoor work and recreation clearly limits the potential to experience the wilder aspects of environment. Viewing selective representations of other countries via the presentations of Disney World and the like removes both the effort and risk of an actual visit. The increasingly popular but vicarious nature of virtual reality is the antithesis of authentic engagement.

Appropriateness

The concept of 'appropriateness' appears to be a guiding concept of much general behaviour and as such fits in well with an ethical account that takes note of context which could, it is argued, be applied to engagement with wilder places. Nevertheless, it is important to distinguish appropriateness, as a well underpinned concept, from the thinner and arguably unfounded class-based notions of 'good form', etiquette and the like. For example, it might be an appropriate ethical act to vacate a seat for someone more infirm than oneself but to do so merely on the basis of their gender would be based upon a much thinner notion.

Constraints wrought by the limitations of psychological and physical abilities, in respect of authentic engagement with environment, may be the ethically soundest way of controlling access to the most vulnerable locations. The notion of appropriateness would, however, allow for adaptations to allow the less able to access some of the less wild places. For example, the provision of wheelchair accessible tracks around relatively humanised landscapes in the English Lake District might be regarded as appropriate but not if laid across the higher and wilder fells of the area.

Guided by the preceding discussion, the following three pairs of examples will be considered in order to clarify instances of varying authenticity and appropriateness of engagement.

Bolt-protected 'sports' climbs compared with the British tradition of leader-placed protection

British rock-climbing has an internal ethic, the practice of which has been based largely upon the use of leader-placed protection,[11] the mode of attachment of running-belays, used to protect the lead climber, being reliant upon natural features in the rock. Originally rope slings were placed over rock spikes or threaded around chock-stones but, in more recent years, this has developed into the practices of fitting wedges and camming-devices[12] into cracks and pockets. Although pitons[13] require an existing crack, there has, historically, been a reluctance to employ them in any widespread way.

All of this can be contrasted with bolt-protected *sport-climbing* which, although present in the UK, is probably best known in the context of French and Spanish limestone climbing. Such climbs are equipped with regularly spaced bolts and a pitch top lowering-off point – usually a chain linking two bolts. Modern versions of these bolts are glued into pre-drilled holes using strong resin glues to produce reliable anchors. Such an approach has undoubtedly encouraged climbing at a technically extremely high standard and those *sport* routes which can be found in the UK are predominantly on very technical ground which could not be protected by leader-placed protection.

On the European continent, however, such an approach is applied across the full spectrum of difficulty. Some argue that bolting climbs is an egalitarian process in that the range of equipment required to participate is reduced and thus the activity is opened up to the less well-off. In parts of France the provision of *sport* climbs is regarded as a pull for visiting tourists and local *syndicats d'initiative* subsidise the cost of bolting. Such a commodification can also be witnessed in the high Alps where bolts have been placed to ease the lot of professional guides looking after their fee-paying clients.

Clearly, although a greater range of gadgets is employed, one can appreciate that leader-placed protection meets Nature much more on its own terms than does bolt-protection. The climber has to relate the range of his technology to the structure of the flakes, threads, cracks and pockets that occur naturally in the rock. In contrast a bolt- hole can be drilled virtually anywhere. Although repeated use of leader-placed protection can polish the sides of cracks, such technology is usually removed by the second and is not a permanent feature like a bolt. Bolts may also be more permanently damaging when the metal parts or glue end their useful life and it might not be possible to replace the fixing in the same hole.

Although it is not being suggested that bolt-protected climbing is an uninteresting activity,[14] it does, as a result of a less authentic mode of engagement, restrict the range of experience. It is climbing mainly *for the move*. The climber might be able to push his/her technical ability to the limit but, because of the inherent safety of the bolts, the outcome of failure is hardly in doubt, for the length of any fall is limited, on overhanging rock it is likely to be into space, and it is often straightforward to lower to the ground. One of the key elements of a full climbing experience is missing to a great extent – namely the uncertainty of a successful and safe outcome. The process has been sanitised at the expense of limiting the range of possible experience.

In contrast the use of leader-placed protection ensures some doubt as to the outcome and the climber has the added interest of matching her gadgets to the opportunities that the rock provides. It is an enhanced kinaesthetic experience and, also much more of a head-game with the control of fear just as important (perhaps more so on some climbs with limited protection) as physical prowess alone. It is a very different mental experience to lead a well-bolted sports climb compared to a climb with poor quality leader-placed protection. In the former case one only has to make the moves and clip the bolts, whilst in the latter a complexity of possible decisions is presented, typically often about whether to hang around on poor holds to place gear and risk running out of stamina or waiting to reach a resting place before placing gear and risking a longer fall.[15] Such quandaries are presented with the risk of injury giving them a real authenticity.

Bolt-protection is therefore not merely potentially more environmentally damaging than leader-placed protection but its use limits the range and quality of sporting experience for the climber.

Skiing on piste compared to ski-touring

Even if one restricts consideration to those aspects of the downhill skiing scene that are deemed necessary to the sport, rather than the après-ski, namely uplift and the provision of manicured pistes, the environmental impact of the activity is considerably more than that associated with ski-touring.

The creation of a piste sanitises Nature: snow quality is machined to be as uniform as possible; the risk of avalanche is reduced; the effort of climbing is removed; routes are marked and shelter from inclement weather is provided close by.[16] The kinaesthetic experience of piste-based skiing is clearly of some quality, and is popular, but fails to emulate the diversity of that provided by ski-touring. It is not being suggested that piste-based skiing is not an enjoyable and worthwhile sport but that, because of an engagement with Nature which is much less authentic when compared to ski-touring, it is a less full experience in contrast.

Although the personal paraphernalia of the ski-tourer (climbing skins; altimeter; map; compass; avalanche transceiver; shovel; ice axe; crampons, etc.) is greater than that of the piste-based skier it mediates Nature less. All of this technology is used in meeting Nature more on its own terms. In addition to the enhanced kinaesthetic of dealing with a variety of snow types and an enhanced aesthetic of place, the whole experience is broadened. The technology of the ski-tourer is used in an engagement which demands knowledge of Nature and of adaptation to changing circumstances. An appreciation of varying avalanche risk, of avoidance strategies and of an ability to deal with accidents replaces the piste-based approach of machining the snow, providing avalanche fences, dynamiting suspect slopes and the like in order to reduce risk to negligible levels. Rather than the piste-based skier learn about, and adapt to, Nature, conditions are altered to a large extent on his/her behalf.

The growth in popularity of off-piste skiing is clearly, for some at least, bound up in the marketing of so-called extreme sports (and some would add, in the presence of macho posturing). Nevertheless, something of its attraction lies in the fuller experience it offers because of its more authentic engagement with the mountain environment.

Driven grouse shooting compared to individual/small group stalking of wild game

A local variation of the Willow Grouse, the Red Grouse (*Lagopus lagopus scoticus*) is a native bird of the British Isles that breeds naturally on suitable moorland habitat. The shooting of Red Grouse as conducted on the heather moorlands of England and Scotland is an excellent example of an inauthentic 'sporting' engagement with Nature. The focus of such shooting appears to be an obsession with the size of *bag*, i.e. the quantity of game that has been killed.

On British sporting estates human intervention via game management is aimed at producing populations of British Red Grouse in far higher densities than would occur naturally. To this end, extensive, and sometimes illegal, predator control is practised and the moorland vegetation is burned in rotation to produce a mosaic of different aged heather (which the species prefers) in almost mono-culture vegetation. Grit that is provided for the birds, as they use it to aid digestion, may contain added medication, to counter the various parasites and ailments to which the grouse are prone especially in high-density populations. Although the area of heather moorland in the UK has diminished markedly over the last fifty years and is, arguably,[17] of conservation importance to a number of wading and other birds, predator management is bad news for most raptors. It is difficult to regard the management of grouse moors (especially when combined with over-grazing by sheep) as being ecologically benign when *all* aspects are considered.

The shooting itself is usually conducted with the shooters aligned at a series of butts, whilst the birds are driven over them by a team of beaters. Although the birds fly rapidly, and thus some shooting skill is retained, the whole process, with its emphasis on the success of a large *bag*, is reduced in quality for the keen marksman. Again we have an example of an inauthentic activity that elicits a diminished quality of sporting experience.

It seems that those engaged in the self-reliant stalking of wild game, occurring at natural levels of density, are pursuing an activity which engages with Nature more authentically and as a result holds the potential to be a qualitatively better 'sporting' experience. For example, one might think of shooters that have been met whilst ski-touring on the upland plateaux of Norway. They have demonstrated a self-reliant approach in a potentially hostile environment, travelled by foot or ski and appeared to have taken great pleasure from the occasional kill resulting from careful stalking.

Compare this approach to that of the English or Scottish grouse moor where shooters are typically delivered close to their allotted butt by vehicle, where shelter from the weather is often provided in the form of a building in which a catered lunch is served. The whole enterprise is organised by the estate staff and the individual shooter need bring little to the exercise barring some ability to aim and fire a shotgun safely. It is hardly surprising to note that such shooting is sometimes marketed as corporate entertainment.[18]

Although the writer finds it hard to empathise with the notion of shooting animals as sport, it does not take much imagination to accept driven grouse shooting as the less satisfying experience of the two. The formulator of the Land Ethic, the seminal conservationist and environmental philosopher Aldo Leopold (himself once engaged in the academic study of and practice in game stock predator control), was scathing in his condemnation of forms of shooting, in particular of British grouse shooting, in which engagement with Nature is overly mediated.[19]

The possibility of an enhanced aesthetic?

The Romantic Movement took consideration of wild places, especially mountains, beyond the purely instrumental assessment of earlier generations. Previously, wild places had been assessed for their instrumental value as sources of economic gain, and, often lacking in such potential, they were usually regarded negatively.[20]

Although Romanticism represented a major sea-change in attitude, with its emphasis on the aesthetic qualities of Nature, the paradigms it provided were hardly authentic: the formulaic composition of the Picturesque and, in practice, the largely disengaged appreciation of the Sublime. The former is the epitome of a disengaged landscape aesthetic – viewing a vista from a fixed location as if it were a framed picture in an art gallery. The latter may suggest a more engaged interaction with features that, seemingly beyond comprehension, engendered feelings of awe and danger, but a reading of contemporary accounts suggests that much of this appreciation took place from a distance and from places of relative safety. It was still a form of predominantly visual landscape aesthetic, not an aesthetic based on a genuine immersion in the locality.

Although not usually in language that is redolent of aesthetic theory, the more recent writings of those who undertake sports in wild places often mention, if not in name, an enhanced aesthetic, especially kinaesthetic, experience derived from adventure in such locations. As Mortlock (2001: 88) puts it succinctly: 'there is a distinction between being in a wild place and looking at a view'.

Berleant's (1997) multi-sensory *aesthetics of engagement* provides a possible basis on which to build a theory of an enhanced aesthetic experience derived from appropriate and authentic sporting engagement with wilder places. His theory replaces the detached and predominantly visual landscape type of aesthetic theory with one based upon multi-sensory, located engagement. A regard for authenticity is suggested in Berleant's writing, especially in an excellent deconstructional critique of Disney World. Giving authenticity greater emphasis and combining it with the notion of appropriateness could add to Berleant's concept of a multi-sensory engaged aesthetic to provide a workable theory which could underpin the best of actuality in practice. Furthermore, such a theory disregards any mind/body dualism and its more monistic approach surely resonates with sporting experience.

In conclusion

Nature could never be the sole and absolute guide to our conduct in wild places. To posit such a view would be to deny ourselves as the technology-employing animals that we are. Since humans started to employ the simplest of technologies, our interface with Nature has not solely been on Nature's own terms but has been mediated to some extent. If, however, one accepts the central argument of this chapter – that sound anthropocentric and ecocentric reasoning force us to revision sporting interface with wilder places – then it suggests that man should be *guided* by authentic and appropriate engagement with Nature on its own terms. Some Aristotelian type of balance-seeking in ethical decision-making may well represent a useful approach, whereby human sporting activity in wilder places is still *guided* by Nature *largely* on its own terms but which has room to admit *honestly* something of the reality of technology in the life of the modern human. Just as the concept of wilderness as an absolute one has been criticised above, it would be a similar mistake to apply the ideas of authentic and appropriate engagement absolutely too. A key objective for adventure sports is the imaginative and aesthetically pleasing use of technology so that the possibility of a complex, multi-sensory and fulfilling engagement with Nature becomes more likely while keeping in check sports' negative environmental impact.[21]

Notes

1 Material informing this chapter was presented previously to a seminar at the Institute for Environment, Philosophy and Public Policy at Lancaster University, and an earlier version read at the 31st Annual Meeting of the International Association for the Philosophy of Sport, at the University of Gloucestershire. The writer wishes to acknowledge the constructive feedback offered by participants at both events.
2 For UK figures see graphical representation in Parker and Meldrum (1973).
3 See, for example, Price *et al.* (2002) for an indication of the extent and economic importance of outdoor recreation to Scotland.

4 The usual 'the' before 'environment' has been discarded, after Berleant (1997), to emphasise the lack of discontinuity between humans and the rest of environment.

5 See Callicott and Nelson (1998) for a comprehensive collection both supporting and critical of the concept of wilderness.

6 See, for example, Denevan (1998).

7 For a comparison of the Anglo-Welsh cultural landscape and North American wilderness models of landscape designation see Dougherty (2005).

8 See Mitchell (1998).

9 Such an approach has been suggested by a few leading mountaineers. See Simpson (1997).

10 See, for example, the National Trust for Scotland (2002) *Wild Land Policy*. The long walk in principle encapsulates the notion that if a climbing ground is located away from the road-head then the climber should expect to cover that distance under his own steam. He should neither expect nor seek mechanised assistance (excepting in certain circumstances a bicycle) or other facilities, such as laid footpaths or bridges, that might ease his approach. In putting emphasis on individual willingness to effort, skill and fitness, the application of this principle results in a degree of self-selection – the more distant locations are less frequently visited and thus their carrying capacity is less likely to be exceeded. The principle is regarded by many in the climbing community as ethically much more defensible than either a permit quota system or the levying of charges.

11 That is placed ground-up by the first climber and removed by the last climber on the rope – the team progressing from start to finish of the route. In contrast, bolted sports climbs are often equipped from abseil and the route practised in stages – the route remains equipped permanently for the lifetime of the bolts.

12 Often referred to by the generic term *Friend*, this is a device which can be fitted quickly into existing cracks – it has several pairs of cams which can be retracted by pulling a trigger and then placed so as to expand and grip the rock. In contrast to previously available equipment, camming-devices can be used in parallel-sided cracks, and even ones which flare outwards, and have thus greatly increased the potential for leader-placed protection.

13 Pitons are metal spikes of varying design that can be hammered into a variety of crack sizes. Rock-climbers in the UK rarely carry a hammer and pitons are little used here in summer conditions. They are still used in winter climbing when: (1) safe alternatives may be hard to find; (2) the above-mentioned camming-devices can be unreliable in iced-up cracks; and (3) one of the pair of ice axes carried usually has a hammer-head.

14 See, for example, George (2006) for an up-to-date evocation of the delights of Scottish sport climbing.

15 This particular quandary was marked especially in steep ice-climbing because traditional ice-screws were hard to place. It was certainly an activity in which the predominantly physical was eclipsed by the difficulty of emotional control. Although this is still true to a large extent, modern ice-screw designs now allow for speedy and efficient, one-handed placement.

16 Whilst many might consider these managements as providing goods of the sport, it nevertheless is the case that these are examples of Nature being sanitised.

17 See, for example, Brown and Bainbridge (1995: 51) 'Grouse moors have been instrumental in protecting uplands from forestry and agricultural intensification, but important populations of many upland species are found on moorland managed for other purposes. Very few, if any, species are dependent on grouse moors *per se*.'

18 For those more familiar with stadium-located team games, it might be helpful, in this context, to note calls, prior to their World Cup, from quarters within USA soccer suggesting bigger goals so that there would be greater scores and thus *more excitement like basketball*. Such a call, seemingly lacking a deep appreciation for the intricacies of the game, could be seen to have parallels in the discussion regarding shooting.

19 See Leopold (1968).
20 See, for example, Defoe (1971).
21 Drasdo (1973) is an early and significant contribution to the analysis of the multi-sensory aesthetic of adventure mountain sports, especially rock-climbing.

References

Berleant, A. (1997) *Living in the Landscape – Toward an Aesthetics of Environment*, Kansas: University Press of Kansas.
Brown, A. F. and Bainbridge, I. P. (1995) 'Grouse Moors and Upland Breeding Birds', in D. B. A. Thompson and A. J. Hester and M. B. Usher (eds.) *Heaths and Moorland: Cultural Landscapes*, Edinburgh: HMSO.
Callicott, J. B. and Nelson, M. P. (eds.) (1998) *The Great New Wilderness Debate*, Athens: The University of Georgia Press.
Defoe, D. (1971) *A Tour Through the Whole Island of Great Britain*, Harmondsworth: Penguin. (First published 1724–6.)
Denevan, W. M. (1998) 'The Pristine Myth: The Landscape of the Americas in 1492', in J. B. Callicott and M. P. Nelson (eds.), *The Great New Wilderness Debate*, Athens: University of Georgia Press.
Dougherty, A. P. (2005) 'Two Models of National Parks: Ethical and Aesthetic Issues in Management Policy for Mountain Regions', in D. B. A. Thompson, M. F. Price and C. A. Galbraith (eds.) *The Mountains of Northern Europe: Conservation, Management, People and Nature*, Edinburgh: Scottish Natural Heritage/The Stationery Office.
Drasdo, H. (1973) *Education and the Mountain Centres*, Llanrwst: Published privately.
George, J. (2006) 'Sportingly Scottish', *Climb Magazine*, 21 (November), Kettering: Greenshires Publishing.
Guignon, C. (2004) *On Being Authentic*, London: Routledge.
Leopold, A. (1968) *A Sand County Almanac and Sketches Here and There*, New York: Oxford University Press. (First published 1949.)
Mitchell, I. (1998) *Scotland's Mountains before the Mountaineers*, Edinburgh: Luath Press.
Mortlock, C. (2001) *Beyond Adventure*, Milnthorpe: Cicerone Press.
Parker, T. M. and Meldrum, K. I. (1973) *Outdoor Education*, London: Dent.
Price, M. F., Dixon, B. J., Warren, C. R. and Macpherson, A. R. (2002) *Scotland's Mountains: Key Issues for their Future Management*, Battleby: Scottish Natural Heritage.
Simpson, J. (1997) *Dark Shadows Falling*, London: Vintage.

9 Outline of a phenomenology of snowboarding

Sigmund Loland

Introduction

In the 1960s, an American surfer, Sherman Poppen, developed what he called the 'snurfer', a kind of a single water ski for use on snow with a traction pad on the middle and a rope fastened at the front. The device was primitive and gave little control, and the rides were risky. The snurfer was developed further by skiing and surfing enthusiasts such as Tom Sims, Dimitrije Milovich and Jake Burton Carpenter. By the end of the 1970s, the snowboard had found its form more or less. In the mid- and late 1980s, stimulated by further technical innovations and by a televised world-wide professional tour starting in 1986–7, snowboarding developed into one of the main sport subcultures among young people. In the mid-1990s, an estimated 2 million people snowboarded all over the world. Perhaps surprisingly, more snowboards were sold than alpine skis.

Gradually, the phenomenon of snowboarding caught academic, commercial and professional interest. Its immense growth led to the establishment of snowboarding schools and to the development of various instructional materials. Snowboarding technique was analysed from the perspectives of pedagogy and didactics, and to a certain extent within biomechanical frameworks (Reichenfeld and Bruechert, 1995; Fabbro, 1996; Svensk Utförsåkning, 1998). The instructional and scientific material provides good descriptions of the elements of snowboarding technique and how to learn it. However, the descriptions may seem narrow in the sense that they offer little or no understanding of the *esprit* of snowboarding in terms of its values and the reasons for its success. These latter topics have been pursued by sports sociologists, anthropologists, and ethnographers alike. Scholars such as Humphreys (1997), Anderson (1999), Heino (2000) and Christensen (2001), to name a few, understand snowboarding as part of a late modern or post-modern youth subculture, and as (healthy) opposition to highly organized, institutionalized and standardized competitive sport. Moreover, with popular films and images of radical descents in deep snow by snowboarding icons such as Craig Kelly and Terje Haakonsen, the sport has been linked closely to values such as freedom and individualism, risk and adventure.

Accounts of the biomechanical and pedagogical aspects of snowboarding are crucial in the education of instructors and important in the learning of the sport. Studies of its socio-cultural importance help the interpretation and understanding of the phenomenon and provide much needed critical perspectives on a rapidly growing sport. To a certain extent, the two perspectives seem to complement each other. Still, they can be criticized for not taking seriously some of the key features of the phenomenon of snowboarding *per se*. Within biomechanics, there is no room for expressions often used by snowboarders referring to experiential qualities such as 'joy', 'flow' and 'rhythm'. Similarly, social scientists have to a certain extent overlooked unique characteristics of the very practising of snowboarding and interpreted the sport as a typical expression of more general processes of modern society. In a discussion of so-called board sports (surfing, skateboarding and snowboarding), Heino (2000: 175) states that 'the stronger connection is not in technique but in the resistance of their predominantly youth cultures to the dominant culture'.

The aim of this chapter is to sketch an approach to snowboarding that seems less theoretically and methodologically fixed and more open to interpretations of the activity in itself. More specifically, I will offer a phenomenological account of the sport. First, to indicate the perspective adopted, I list some rather loose theoretical and methodological premises. Second, I outline some key points in a phenomenology of snowboarding free-riding technique, the most open and adventurous form of the sport. In the third and concluding section, I reflect upon how phenomenological analyses may provide a starting point for other scholarly analyses of snowboarding in particular and sporting activities in general.

Phenomenology of movement

The phenomenological approach has roots in a reaction against what was considered a distanced and scientistic approach towards human conduct and experience, especially as found in the psychology of the late nineteenth and early twentieth centuries. The aim of the founding father of philosophical phenomenology, Edmund Husserl, was to analyse human intention 'in itself' (Bell, 1991). Husserlian phenomenology is occupied with exploring the basic structures of consciousness, or, more specifically, the basic structures of human intentionality. A key phenomenological thesis is that human consciousness is always deliberately and purposely directed in a very fundamental way – it is always 'consciousness of something'. From this premise, phenomenologists proceed and study the *noema*, or 'that which presents itself to consciousness'. Husserl's methodological advice was to go *zu den Sachen*, to the things in themselves. Through a phenomenological reduction (*Epoche*), an intentional act in which prejudices and previous knowledge are 'bracketed', the essence of an experiential structure can be intuitively grasped and isolated. Through systematic reflection and 'free, imaginative variation' (another methodological slogan among phenomenologists), the researcher can bring to light its hidden meanings and qualities.

These premises need not be understood in essentialistic terms. The aim of this chapter is not to establish some kind of pure phenomenology, or to try to grasp 'the essence' or 'true nature' of snowboarding. Obviously, human practices cannot be isolated and analysed independent of their social and cultural contexts. Nevertheless, my thesis is that in studies of snowboarding (as of many other sports), embodied practice, that is, the sport as 'lived' from the practitioner's point of view, is easily overlooked. In a phenomenological account, lived, embodied experience is given epistemological primacy as a mode of access to the real. French philosopher Maurice Merleau-Ponty writes:

> I am my body, at least wholly to the extent that I possess experience, and yet at the same time my body is as it were a 'natural' subject, a provisional sketch of my whole being. This experience of one's own body runs counter to the reflective procedure which detaches subject and object from each other, and which gives us only the thought about the body, or the body as an idea, or not the experience of the body or the body in reality.
>
> (Merleau-Ponty, 1962: 198–9)

In what follows, a snowboarder is understood as embodied, intentional consciousness that interacts with the world in dialectic, meaning-producing ways. The interaction can take many forms. In successful runs, riders seem to transcend traditional distinctions between body, equipment and environment, and experience the very doing of snowboarding as one unified, meaningful whole. Snowboarders move as body-subjects. As will be argued below, such 'peak experiences' (to use a classic Maslowian term) can only be understood on phenomenological premises. In other situations, snowboarders can experience their riding in more objective, distanced and almost mechanical ways. In technical training, for instance, riders may examine critically the efficiency of alternative weight distribution on the board, or the angle of their ankles and knees while turning. And sometimes the body-object experience is due to the gaze of others and coloured by the socio-cultural norms of appearance and movement in the sport.

It is to this 'life world' (*Lebenswelt*) of snowboarding I now turn. After having narrowed the analysis to snowboard free-riding. I will outline its basic technical movement patterns, also called technical elements, as articulated by the experienced rider or instructor and as expressed in instructional material such as that of Reichenfeld and Bruechert (1995), Fabbro (1996) and Svensk Utförsåkning (1998). The analysis will be informed by didactic and mechanical knowledge in the field but in selective and 'superficial' ways, as my focus will really be on 'lived practice'. The raw material for the 'free, imaginative variation' is the way snowboarders experience and talk of their sport. Following this, I will examine how skilled snowboarding can be understood as a holistic experience in which technical elements come together in unified wholes.

Snowboarding styles

Snowboarding includes a variety of styles and riding patterns. Somewhat simplistically, we can talk of three styles: the alpine, the freestyle and the free-ride.

Inspired by alpine skiing, alpine snowboarding values the carved turn on well-prepared surfaces in which the front and the back of the board follow the same track without skidding. In its extreme versions, this is a slalom-race technique. Alpine snowboarding holds an ambiguous place in the snowboarding culture as it is placed between skiing (which to many snowboarders is 'the enemy'), and the freestyle and free-ride styles described below.

Freestyle is quite different and includes the half pipe, and aerial and trick manoeuvres. From the mass media and popular culture point of view, freestyle is the iconographic snowboarding style. The free-ride is less strictly defined. Free-riding borrows elements from both alpine and freestyle techniques and is the all-round style for various terrains and slopes. It includes skills in turning and jumping on firm surfaces, in *off-piste* deep snow, and in steeps and jumps. Extreme free-riding involves risky, steep descents with high-speed turns and acrobatic jumps in virgin terrain. To restrict the analysis somewhat, the phenomenological sketch will be linked to the basic technical elements involved since they are the necessary building blocks upon which to master all other challenges of the sport.

Good equilibrium conditions: gliding in a balanced position

Together with surfing, skating and skiing, snowboarding includes the particular experiential quality of *gliding* on the surface. Gliding sports remove the harshness of gravity and represent contrasts to universal and common movement patterns such as walking, running and jumping. Gliding poses particular challenges to states of equilibrium. Mechanically speaking, a body is in equilibrium when the result of all force vectors acting on it equals zero. In stable equilibrium conditions the force vector acting from a body's point of gravity and towards the centre of the earth falls within its supporting base. Gliding on an uneven surface implies constant challenges in this respect. To the unskilled snowboarder, instability is experienced as threats of falling. To stabilize, arms, upper body and hips move dramatically and are often, to a certain degree at least, uncontrolled. The skilled snowboarder moves in and out of stable equilibrium conditions in a controlled, playful manner and with a minimum of energy expenditure.

The key to good equilibrium conditions is the position on the board. Due to the limited snowboard width, adopting a sideways position is a matter of necessity. To enable easier and more flexible weight distribution, the distance between the forward and backward foot is about the width of the hips. Knees and hips are flexed to lower the point of gravity and reduce the distance to the supporting base. Arms are relaxed but slightly stretched and work as balance adjustments just like the balance pole of the line dancer. The front shoulder and arm are pointing towards the line of travel.

If a snowboarder is able to meet the mechanical requirements of good equilibrium conditions, he or she is in good balance. Good balance is the experiential, phenomenological equivalent to good equilibrium conditions. As with bicycling, the supporting base of the turning snowboarder is sometimes marginal. On hard surfaces, when the board is tipped on its edge the rider balances on a steel edge a few millimetres wide and approximately 1.5 metres long. The challenge to the rider is to utilize centripetal forces (forces acting from the centre of gravity and towards the centre of the circle of which the turn is a part) while at the same time working on stable equilibrium conditions. Expert riders do this in creative and playful ways. Balancing on the edge of the board while not moving is impossible. Just as in bicycling, a fundamental quality of snowboarding is constant, dynamic and well-balanced movements. Snowboarding is a sport in which one is constantly 'on the move'.

Snowboarders' solutions to balance challenges are diverse. Most riders use their left foot forward (*regular* style), although a few prefer to ride with the right foot forward (*goofy* style). One method for establishing one's style is by determining which foot one prefers when kicking a ball; or which foot one puts forward when one is pushed from behind in order to re-establish balance; or which foot one prefers putting first when sliding on a slippery surface. The angle of the feet towards the line of travel is, at least to a certain extent, a matter of individual preference, too. Snowboard bindings are adjustable at the level of 1 degree. (The rule of thumb is to find a front foot angle that feels comfortable – in free riding, 20–40 degrees – and then adjust the rear foot accordingly – usually 15–35 degrees.)

The position on the board is not strictly defined but is found in a rather open trial-and-error process. Snowboarding seems to build on intuitive and basic movement patterns. Moreover, the sideways position is a quite radical alternative to conventional, symmetrical sport techniques in which the body fronts the direction of travel. This holds true even for related gliding sports such as alpine skiing, water skiing and speed skating.

Good equilibrium conditions and the experience of being in good balance are the *conditio sine qua non* of snowboarding. In the basic position, a snowboarder is at the centre of all possible movement patterns on the board: backwards and forwards, sideways, and upwards and downwards. Yet good positioning is a necessary but by no means a sufficient condition for successful snowboarding. Further key skills are the controlling of speed and direction.

Manipulating friction: controlling speed and direction

As in all gliding sports, snowboarding includes techniques for the efficient regulation of speed and direction. According to Newton's law of inertia, a body continues in a state of rest, or in uniform motion in a straight line, except and in so far as it may be compelled by external forces to change that state. To be able to change speed and direction, snowboarders have to manipulate friction. In mechanical terms, this means mainly manipulating resistance forces acting between the board and the snow and in the opposite direction of the line of travel. Technically good riders use frictional forces in balanced and efficient ways. Controlling speed and direction is achieved primarily by the 'edging' of the board in relation to the surface.

Edging means rolling the board from edge to edge or balancing it on one of its edges. Putting a board on its edge makes it skid and brake, and/or turn. Snowboards are designed originally for turns in soft snow. Their cut is narrow on the middle and with wide fronts and tails. When the board is fully balanced on its edge, it carves a turn with a radius that equals the circle of which the cut of the board constitutes a part. When edging, the area of contact between the board and the snow is reduced. Frictional forces between the board and the surface increase, and the rider can change direction. The more the angle of the edge towards the snow is increased, and/or the more pressure is put on the board, the stronger are the frictional forces created resulting in sharper turns.

There are many ways of achieving edging. The initiating movement is called 'pivoting'. Pivoting refers to the steering of the board by putting weight on the front foot, and by kicking the rear foot forward or backward. The movement implies rotating the lower body including the hips while keeping the torso rather stable. Due to the sideways position, and in contradistinction to gliding sports with symmetrical movement patterns such as alpine skiing, the snowboarder utilizes two edging and turning techniques.

The heelside turn implies putting the board on its backside edge by 'lifting the toes' and pushing the hips backwards. Balance is adjusted by leaning the upper body outwards and down the hill. At high speeds, the whole body can be leant inwards with the arms stretched forwards to adjust balance. Often, this is the first turn to be mastered as it overlaps with creating friction to reduce speed (heelside sideslipping). It feels relatively safe: riders can fall backwards and still be in control.

In the toeside turn, the rider 'climbs up' on their toes to put the board on its inner edge. Knees and ankles are bent and ready for flexible adjustments. In short turns, the bending of knees and ankles is sufficient to roll from heelside to toeside edge and back. The torso is kept relatively stable. In long turns at high speeds, the rider leans inwards in the turn with the whole body. Although instructional materials describe the toeside turn as the easier one, the turn takes certain courage as the rider has the back towards downhill and no good overview of potential falling zones. When in balance, however, the toeside turn is an extraordinarily stable and powerful turn.

When executed well, and with good balance, heelside and toeside edging leads to carving turns – the classic sign of a skilled rider. In a carving turn, the front and the back of the board follow the same even and clean line on the surface with a minimum of sideways drift and skidding. On soft snow turning takes a minimum of edging, on hard surfaces edging has to be radical, in both instances skilled riding requires a delicate balancing of forces. This implies a close and finely adjusted balance and use of force.

Long turns at highs speeds have a particular floating quality to them. Characteristically, this kind of snowboarding is called *cruising* (see Figure 9.1). The carving turn on firm surface and the well-balanced turn in deep snow are the fastest and most efficient turns in snowboarding. But cruising with smooth yet at the same time decisive and carving turns poses radical technical challenges. A key skill in this respect is the linking together of turns.

Figure 9.1 Cruising. Observe how the rider is balanced in the sideways position, how the board is edged from heelside to toeside turns, and how turns are linked together with smooth weighting and unweighting technique.

Linking turns together: weighting and unweighting techniques

A gradual increase of edging indicates the initiation of a turn which again (according to the Newtonian third law of reaction) results in increased friction and an equally strong counterforce from the surface. As the snowboarder crosses the fall line, the centripetal force that keeps the rider in the curve and hence the frictional forces towards the surface, have to be increased. To achieve this, good riders utilize a technique that is most often explained with references to the Newtonian law of intertia: pressure control, or weighting and un-weighting technique.

The first part of a turn does not require much friction. The rider stands in an upright position, the lead shoulder points in the desired direction, and the weight is put forwards allowing pivoting with the rear foot to let the front of the board drift into the fall line of the hill. The rider works *with* gravitational forces. As the rider approaches the crossing of the fall line, there is need for a gradual work against the components of the gravitational force that acts downwards in the hill. To stay in the turn, sideways frictional forces have to be increased. The good rider does this by creating centripetal forces acting from his or her centre of gravity and towards the centre of the circle of which the curve is a part.

In the first half of the turn, the centre of gravity is gradually lowered by flexing ankles, knees and hips, and the body is gradually compressed. The movement looks almost as a slow-motion preparation for a jump. When crossing the fall line, good riders heighten the centre of gravity and rise. Due to the law of intertia, the result is the same as in a jump or a rapid upwards movement. There will be a much needed increase in frictional forces between the board and the snow. The board is weighted. If it is balanced on its edge, the result is a powerful, carving completion of the turn.

At the completion of the turn, the rider is in an upright position, and (again due to the law of inertia) frictional forces decrease. Now the rider is in an un-weighted phase. The rider can pivot into a new direction almost without effort, and a new weighting phase is initiated followed by a new compression and gradual rise of the body.

Good snowboarders master the technical elements of snowboarding and link together turns into harmonious chains. In skilful *cruising*, the rolling from toe to heel and backwards is done with a sweeping movement of the hips that provides strong sensual and kinaesthetic pleasures. In wild and steep *off-piste* terrain, snowboard free-riding is an epitome of an adventure sport. Good riders play with gravity – they have what is often referred to as 'board feeling' or good snowboarding rhythm.

Snowboarding rhythm

Rhythm comes from Greek *rhythmos* with the general meaning of a dynamic, floating, modifiable form. Most definitions of rhythm refer to the perception of the meaningful ordering of elements in time and space.[1] In sport and other motor activities, rhythm seems to refer to an intelligible and meaningful order of movement elements. How can rhythm be further operationalized in the snowboarding context?

In a phenomenologically inspired part of their movement analysis, Meinel and Schnabel (1987: 92–111) talk of phase structures, that is, of movement sequences that appear to be 'natural' wholes and in which all significant technical elements of a sport are represented. Most sports have rhythmic phase structures that occur in a repetitive pattern. Meinel and Schnabel refer to such phases being distinguished by, for example, regular repetitions of effort-relaxation, stretch-bow, right-left, and so on. In running, the basic phase structure is a step, in swimming a stroke, and in snowboarding a heelside and toeside turn. The intelligible and meaningful tying together of single turns into chains of turns make up what can be referred to as a particular snowboarding rhythm.

I have written of the technical elements of snowboarding in both mechanical (equilibrium conditions, friction, weighting and unweighting) and phenomenological (experiences of being in balance, of edging and pivoting, and of carving turns) terms. From the mechanical point of view, technical elements are seen as meristic wholes;[2] wholes that can be fully analysed and causally explained by looking at their parts. The thesis here is that this is not the case with the unifying principle of technical elements that binds them together into skilled snowboard riding: rhythm. Rhythm is understood as qualitative characteristics of movement patterns that are more than the mere sum of their parts; they are holistic entities that can only be rendered meaningful as experiential wholes. In successful rides, snowboarders do not 'have' a body, rather they 'are' their bodies, to paraphrase the philosopher Marcel (1979). Analysing snowboarding turns as meristic wholes can be done biomechanically and with a view of the moving body as an objective system of forces in interaction with the forces of the environment. In rhythmic movement, snowboarders appear as 'intentional I's' in the phenomenological sense of the word: as pure body subjects.

Dreyfus and Dreyfus (1986) have developed a five-stage model in which the development of skills is described from novice to the expert. At the first four stages, skills can be explained more or less mechanistically with references to rule following and automatization. The fifth expert level, however, is described as qualitatively different.

> An expert generally knows what to do based on mature and practiced under-standing. When deeply involved in coping with his environment, he does not see problems in some detached way and work at solving them, nor does he worry about the future and device plans . . . An expert's skill has become so much a part of him that he need be no more aware of it than he is of his own body.
>
> (Dreyfus and Dreyfus, 1986: 30)

Good snowboarders, it is often said, move 'on intuition' and 'without thinking'. Expert snowboarding is kinetic knowledge unfolding as a dynamic, qualitative flow. The movement rhythm of the expert can only be fully understood as experienced and 'lived'.

Indeed, these ideas are found in more or less well-articulated forms among snowboarders. In most of the instructional material of the sport, there is an emphasis on its joys and excitement, and on its intuitive and 'natural' character. In more esoteric writings, such as Lenz's *Snowboarding to Nirvana* (1997), there is an emphasis on the experience of oneness: the rider, the board, the slope and the mountain are all parts of one force. In the movies and tales of snowboarders such as Terje Haakonsen and Shaun White, the objective and exact aspects of the performance draw little attention. What constitute meaning are the transcending and adventurous characteristics. Rhythm is a sign of an expert's mastery of a skill.

Snowboarding technique: a phenomenological model

Based on what is said above, technical elements of snowboarding can be ordered in an overview or a phenomenological model (see Figure 9.2). From novice to expert levels, snowboarders are challenged on equilibrium conditions, or good balance, linked to a good positioning on the board. Moreover, snowboarding implies a constant need to manipulate friction in terms of pivoting and toeside and heelside edging. The third element is carving, meaning the creation of suffi-cient centripetal force while balancing on the edge of the board to make turns without skidding. The unifying principle, rhythm, is seen to be a key charac-teristic of expert skills and refers to how all these technical elements interact. Different from the other technical elements, movement rhythm is understood as a holistic unity and described in pure experiential or phenomenological terms only.

Nowhere has sport been more assiduously aligned with the electronic media than in the incorporation of extreme and action sport as the ubiquitous, mainstream, dominant sport. Even football, baseball, and basketball, while deeply aligned with television, have retained recognizable large parts of their design; action sports have, in a sense, been defined by ESPN's X Games and NBC's Gravity Games, and the artistic ethos of some of the extreme activities has been modified and changed forever (Rinehart, 1998a).[6]

As Leanne Stedman has suggested in her study of surf culture and feminism, the process of postmodernization has created some dramatically different formations even within 'sports' that have been around for dozens of years. She points out two negative consequences of the postmodernization process as they relate to women in surfing culture: 'accelerated individualization' and 'hyper-commodification'. These two significant arms of the process reflect, respectively, 'smaller niches and [the opening up of surfing] to a multitude of subject positions' and a challenge to 'group cohesion by opening the symbols of the surfing subculture to mass consumption' (Stedman, 1997: 75).

Certainly, Stedman's analysis of surfing culture makes valid points in terms of why surfing, as most sports, is in the process of postmodernization. Cultural conservative Daniel Bell may be correct in noting that the 'postmodern culture of the 1960s was [not] in any way radical or revolutionary, [Bell] calling it "counterfeit culture" that produced little culture and countered nothing' (cited in Dickens, 1994: 85). Similarly, Stedman points out that surfers have reacted negatively to any perceived entry by females into their symbolic spaces, and that they are not, in fact, transformative but rather, conservative and regressive in their use of sport as a vehicle for social justice. The ethos of surfing, particularly the emphasis on surfers carving out cultural niches for themselves, Stedman laments, has reduced rather than increased females' participatory opportunities. Indeed, women are more actively excluded from surfing as counter politically-correct positions are sought by male surfers. As the male surfers reterritorialize the grounds of surfing, so too have many white adolescent males in action sports been drawn toward what Faludi (1991) calls 'backlash' against females attempting to enter 'their' sports. Their exclusion of females (or the other) may serve as a manifestation of their desire to recapture outlaw status, according to Stedman.

It is debatable whether surfing should be considered an action/extreme sport or a mainstream sport. Surfing engages both male and female participants simultaneously, unlike many of the mainstreamed sports. The distinction Stedman draws for surfing, that male surfers feel a need to recapture their own 'outsider' status, certainly aligns with a postmodernist sensibility, however.

Beal (1996) has explored a similar dynamic within pre-adolescent skateboarding culture. The desire to reject mainstream cultural values is strong within the skateboarders she studied, and aligns with a rejection of adult authority and a strong attraction to individual styles. In fact, one skater said that 'there are different styles of skating and all of them are accepted unlike football which he felt that a participant would be kicked off the team for having a different style of play' (Beal, 1996: 209). Such individual learning styles, as Alkemeyer (2002) points out, have the potential to lead to self-enlightenment (or, to self-authority). However, male skaters, like Stedman's surfers, Beal notes, simultaneously embrace stereotypical masculine styles and reject female participation. They tend to attribute the paucity of female skaters to naturalized causes: females 'don't want to get bruised to learn' and 'skating "is a rough sport where people get scarred, and girls don't want to have scars on their shins, it wouldn't look good"' (Beal, 1996: 214).

At the same time, skaters and other extreme/action sports participants have gradually been drawn toward their own reification. Tony Hawk, the skateboarder, has actively pursued his own commodification; so too have other skaters. As an example, Kassak, writing a review of skateboard decks for Big Brother, states,

> I would also love to tell stories of coming up through the amateur contests with the likes of Frank, Chris Pontius . . . Frank Hill and Salman Agah. But I can't because even though I was as good as those guys or maybe a little tiny bit worse, I could never get sponsored.
>
> (Kassak, 2003: 44)

The desire of skaters – and many other action sports participants – to be sponsored by corporations has grown to be endemic within the subculture of action sports (cf. Rinehart, 1998a), and yet, there still remains a nostalgic – and often real – ethos that aligns more closely with Vedantic philosophy. This spur toward celebrity before sporting achievement is somewhat unique in the sporting world – mainstream sports starts certainly achieve celebrity, but generally the process does not begin in low-paying potential of their athleticism like it does within extreme/action sports. This also points to a fluidity of ego-lessness in the grassroots ethos of skating which is gradually being overtaken by the dominant capitalist culture. Yet, 'authentic' skaters – an idealized version – still often display the self-effacing egolessness that is characteristic of the Vedantic philosophy.

The *social* process of postmodernism plays out in action sport in two ways. The overt blending of the forms of sport – mainstream sport, viewed somewhat as high sport, combines with what George Sage (1990) once termed 'trash sport' into new forms of sport that simultaneously embrace mass appeal and high physical skill sets. High sport and low sport can be blended, and there is a recapturing of the sense of play and playful spirit within these new sport forms. Action sport, while highly mediated, still has its antecedents in mass participation, so that wall climbers at the local indoor wall can emulate action sports athletes from the X Games. The sport forms are still approachable and somewhat achievable by everyday humans, and the physical forms these humans take are still rather average. The way that mainstream sports are marketed to consumers approaches unbelievable hype, so that the athletes and the sports themselves have, to some extent, reached untouchable status within sports culture. Many mainstream athletes have little in common with ordinary human beings, but action athletes themselves are still approachable – thus analogous to the high art/low art blend of Sayre's postmodern acts of democratization (1989).

Second, very briefly, action sports have retained their sense of play. Krishnamurti is quite specific in his use of the term 'joy,' and it aligns well with the unselfconscious playfulness of action sports participants:

> You cannot think about joy. Joy is an immediate thing and by thinking about it, you turn it into pleasure. Living in the present is the instant perception of beauty and the great delight in it without seeking pleasure from it.
>
> (Krishnamurti, 1969: 38)

The ethos that youth-driven sport forms (or leisure activity, or lifestyle sports) like action sports brings to the vast array of sports available today is very different from the ethos that mainstream sports brings. Children say, as one informant from Beal's study did, that, 'I like to do stuff that feels cool, that gives me butterflies in my stomach' (Beal, 1996: 210), and a deep sense of play and playfulness is operating.

Process is still key for many of the action sports participants. End-result is only for the very visible, elite members, who, to retain 'authentic' statuses, assume a different kind of 'cool pose' (Majors and Billson, 1992): they fluidly play the corporate game but appear not to care about it.[7]

There is the sense of playful pastiche, the sense of fluidity of subject positionings, within young participants coming up. Their socialization occasionally even suggests that they pay homage to the founders of their sport. For example, writers to skateboarding magazines offer the following ironic diary of their use of a backyard pool (with the owners' permission):

> Sometimes things just fall in our laps, take for example, the Blue Dolphin pool. We get a call from one of our allies that he knows this pool that is getting demo'd and the owners are cool if we come skate it . . . The place was a trip, there was even a 1960's bomb shelter in the backyard. The pool had ladyfinger coping with a super wide perfect tranny that set you up for a ride over the dolphin in the shallow end. We skated it for 7 hours till it got dark and then we rolled out to the bitchen Punk show to go see Narcoleptic Youth.
>
> (Rinehart, 2004: 30–1)

These action sports athletes are youthful themselves. Their values and desires are not mature, yet they open up a window to other youth for the possibilities of self-discovery.

These action sport athletes demonstrate the sense of play, of out-of-bounds 'outsider,' and of what Coakley (2004) terms 'underconformity' to the strictures of normative sport and society. While the successful action sport athletes are organized and dedicated to their craft and art form, they also portray a dynamic sense of resistance. Their very ethos seems to say that they are going to learn and evolve and create new sport forms in anti-authoritarian ways so that they may demonstrate the illusion that they are in control of themselves. In this process of self-discovery, action sports participants demonstrate their alliance with risk and apparent danger and with a disregard for authority. They also, though they may not be reflexive about it, align to some degree with the philosophy of Vedanta, and with the processes of postmodernization.

Notes

1 I am grateful to Becky Beal for discussions that have confused, and, ultimately, clarified many of the issues discussed herein. As well, I am grateful to Suzanne Sutherland for comments and insights that have enhanced the chapter.
2 Coakley also describes a concomitant adherence to 'the sport ethic' to which 'power and performance' participants tend to adhere.
3 Though beyond the scope of this chapter, the cult of celebrity, accruing from athletic exploits, which contributes to a political candidate's name recognition in the United States is an interesting topic. The playout of simplistic decisiveness, which is often not possible in nuanced, real-life situations, contributes to a sense of safety and security – a kind of deliberate infantilization – on the part of constituents so that, intelligence aside, you 'know where he (in most cases it is a he, since sporting women are not celebrated in the same ways as sporting men) stands.' This binary logic, this 'you are either with us or against us' kind of thinking, works well to simplify debates and to reassure the electorate that something is being done – and it is modernist in its antecedents.
4 As an aside, this 'synopsis' technique is itself a very Western approach to knowledge: assuming the ability to encapsulate such a complex array of philosophical knowledge is, of course, impossible. It approximates the impossibility of 'fieldwork' substituting for real insider's knowledge of the Other, and many of the problems with that method of ethnographic research apply to this current project. With that caveat in mind, I shall continue.
5 In fact, in a recent NPR segment, Red Auerbach was quoted as saying that one of the main jobs of NBA basketball in the 1950s and 1960s was to 'promote the game.' With street cred and symbolic capital achieved through a derivative 'cool pose,' action sports athletes have the option to absent themselves from that selling process.
6 Yet localized sites, like Sheshreds, which is run by and for female action sport aficionados, have not become participatory players within the media run that action sports have enjoyed. Though there have been many noises about the egalitarianism of action/extreme sports, female participation at the professional level has been quite limited. As media corporations have begun realizing that they may exploit certain styles of sexualizing action/extreme sports, however, this 'boys-only' attitude has begun to change.
7 With apologies to Richard Majors and J. Billings – this appropriation of the term 'cool pose' coalesces around a sense of white privilege, including concepts of icon-making, the cult of celebrity, and abilities to choose that are quite unlike Majors and Billson's contextualization of the term.
    Kusz (2004: 207) neatly terms white males' uncertainty and resultant backlash 'that "Man With No Name swagger"' and attributes it to their 'whiteness [being] made visible' in extreme sports.

References

Alkemeyer, T. (2002) 'Learning with the Body and the Possibilities of a Practical Reflexivity', *European Journal of Sport Science*, 2(1): 1–9.

Baudrillard, J. (1988) *America*, London: Verso.

Baudrillard, J. (1990) *Cool Memories, 1980–1985*, London: Verso.

Baudrillard, J. (1995) *The Gulf War Did Not Take Place*, Bloomington: Indiana University Press.

Baudrillard, J. (1996) *Cool Memories II, 1987–1990*, Durham, NC: Duke University Press.

Beal, B. (1995) 'Disqualifying the Official: An Exploration of Social Resistance through the Subculture of Skateboarding', *Sociology of Sport Journal*, 12(3): 252–67.

Beal, B. (1996) 'Alternative Masculinity and its Effects on Gender Relations in the Subculture of Skateboarding', *Journal of Sport Behavior*, 19(3): 204–20.

Berger, J., Blomberg, S., Fox, C., Dibb, M., and Hollis, R. (1972) *Ways of Seeing*, London: British Broadcasting Corporation.

Cahn, S. K. (1994) *Coming on Strong: Gender and Sexuality in Twentieth-Century Women's Sport*, New York: Free Press.

Calinescu, M. (1987) *Five Faces of Modernity: Modernism, Avant-Garde, Decadence, Kitsch, Postmodernism*, Durham, NC: Duke University Press.

Coakley, J. (2004) *Sports in Society: Issues and Controversies*, 8th edn, New York: McGraw-Hill.

Coleridge, S. T. (1973) 'Biographica Literaria', in W. Heath (ed.), *Major British Poets of the Romantic Period*, New York: Macmillan.

Csikszentmihalyi, M. (1990) *Flow: The Psychology of Optimal Experience*, New York: Harper & Row.

Dickens, D. R. (1994) 'North American Theories of Postmodern Culture', in D. R. Dickens and A. Fontana (eds.), *Postmodernism and Social Inquiry*, New York: The Guildford Press.

Dunning, E. (1986) 'Sport as a Male Preserve: Notes on the Social Sources of Masculine Identity and its Transformations', in N. Elias and E. Dunning (eds.), *Quest for Excitement: Sport and Leisure in the Civilizing Process*, Oxford: Basil Blackwell.

Easwaran, E. (1987) 'Introduction', in E. Easwaran (trans.), *The Upanishads*, Tomales, CA: The Nilgiri Press.

Elias, N. (1972a) 'The Genesis of Sport as a Sociological Problem', in E. Dunning (ed.), *Sport: Readings from a Sociological Perspective*, Toronto: University of Toronto Press.

Elias, N. (1972b) 'An Essay on Sport and Violence', in N. Elias and E. Dunning, *Quest for Excitement: Sport and Leisure in the Civilizing Process*, Oxford: Basil Blackwell.

ESPN (1995) Broadcast of *The eXtreme Games* (24 June – 3 July), Bristol: CT.

Faludi, S. (1991) *Backlash: The Undeclared War Against American Women*, New York: Crown Books.

Gardels, N. (1992) 'West Turns East at the End of History' (interview with Octavio Paz), *New Perspective Quarterly*, 9: 5–9.

Gillman, P. and Gillman, L. (2000) *The Wildest Dream: The Biography of George Mallory*, Seattle: The Mountaineers Books.

Grey, A. (2001) *The Mission of Art*, Boston: Shambhala.

Guttmann, A. (2004) *Sports: The First Five Millennia*, Amherst: University of Massachusetts Press.

Harper, W. A., Miller, D. M., Park, R. J., and Davis, E. C. (1977) *The Philosophic Process in Physical Education*, 3rd edn, Philadelphia: Lea & Febiger.

Huyssen, A. (1986) *After the Great Divide: Modernism, Mass Culture, Postmodernism*, Bloomington: Indiana University Press.

Jackson, S. A. and Csikszentmihalyi, M. (1999) *Flow in Sports: The Keys to Optimal Experiences and Performances*, Champaign, IL: Human Kinetics.

Kassak, M. (2003) 'Media Skateboards', *Big Brother*, 100: 44.

Krishnamurti, J. (1969) *Freedom from the Known*, ed. M. Lutyens, New York: Harper & Row.

Kusz, K. (2001) '"I Want To Be the Minority": The Cultural Politics of Young White Males in Sport and Popular Culture', *Journal of Sport and Social Issues*, 25(4): 390–416.

Kusz, K. (2004) 'Extreme America: The Cultural Politics of Extreme Sports in 1990s America', in B. Wheaton (ed.), *Understanding Lifestyle Sports: Consumption, Identity and Difference*, London: Routledge.

Lemert, C. (1997) *Postmodernism Is Not What You Think*, Malden, MA: Blackwell Publishers Inc.

Lowe, B. (1977) *The Beauty of Sport: A Cross-Disciplinary Inquiry*, Englewood Cliffs, NJ: Prentice-Hall, Inc.

McPherson, B. D., Curtis, J. E., and Loy, J. W. (1989) *The Social Significance of Sport*, Champaign, IL: Human Kinetics Books.

Majors, R. and Billson, J. M. (1992) *Cool Pose: The Dilemmas of Black Manhood in America*, New York: Touchstone.

Midol, N. (1993) 'Cultural Dissents and Technical Innovations in the "Whiz" Sports', *International Review for the Sociology of Sport*, 28(1): 23–32.

Midol, N. and Broyer, G. (1995) 'Toward an Anthropological Analysis of New Sport Cultures: The Case of Whiz Sports in France', *Sociology of Sport Journal*, 12(2): 204–12.

Paraschak, V. and Rinehart, R. (1995) 'The Universal Singular: Contextualizing the "Other" in Sport Historiography', paper presented at the annual North American Society for Sport History Conference, Long Beach, CA (May).

Rinehart, R. (1995) 'Cyber-Sports: Power and Diversity in ESPN's *The Extreme Games*', paper presented at the annual North American Society for the Sociology of Sport Conference, Sacramento, CA (November).

Rinehart, R. (1998a) 'Inside of the Outside: Pecking Orders within Alternative Sport at ESPN's 1995 *The eXtreme Games*', *Journal of Sport & Social Issues*, 22(4): 398–415.

Rinehart, R. (1998b) *Players All: Performances in Contemporary Sport*, Bloomington: Indiana University Press.

Rinehart, R. (2000) 'Arriving Sport: Alternatives to Formal Sports', in J. Coakley and E. Dunning (eds.), *Handbook of Sport and Society*, London: Sage Publishing, Inc.

Rinehart, R. (2004) 'Team Goon Action Review', *Concrete Wave: 100% Skateboarding*, 3(1): 30–1.

Rinehart, R. and Grenfell, C. (2002) 'BMX Spaces: Children's Grass Roots' Courses and Corporate-Sponsored Tracks', *Sociology of Sport Journal*, 19(3): 302–14.

Sage, G. (1990) *Power and Ideology in American Sport: A Critical Perspective*, Champaign, IL: Human Kinetics Books.

Said, E. W. (1978) *Orientalism*, New York: Pantheon Books.

Sayre, H. M. (1989) *The Object of Performance: The American Avant-Garde since 1970*, Chicago: University of Chicago Press.

Stedman, L. (1997) 'From Gidget to Gonad Man: Surfers, Feminists and Post-modernisation', *The Australian and New Zealand Journal of Sociology*, 33(1): 75–90.

Watts, A. (1966) *The Book: On the Taboo Against Knowing Who You Are*, New York: Vintage Books.

Wheaton, B. (2000) 'Just Do It: Consumption, Commitment and Identity in the Windsurfing Subculture', *Sociology of Sport Journal*, 17(3): 254–74.

Wheaton, B. (ed.) (2004) *Understanding Lifestyle Sports: Consumption, Identity and Difference*, London: Routledge.

11 Extreme sports and the ontology of experience

Ivo Jirásek

Extreme sports

The sports activities that interest us come under various guises: 'extreme', 'high-risk', 'dangerous' or 'hazardous' sports. Despite their frequent use it is not clear what is meant by these terms. Let us suppose that we all understand the word 'sport' the same way: as wilful movement activity especially in the environment of its cultivation.[1] But what about extreme sports? We can consider 'extreme' to refer to everything which is on the periphery; out of the centre (eccentric); extravagant; or done to excess. The old Greek ideal carved out over the entrance of Delphi's oracular shrine, 'Nothing to excess', is not adhered to in the case of extreme sports. The advantage of thinking of 'extreme' sports in this way, however, is the enlarged perception and understanding of some characteristics or developmental tendencies of the investigated phenomena; and it has a corollary in politics: the middle is a mixture of liberal and social positions. We distinguish essentially two profiles from this central point: left (socialist) and right (conservative). Areas away from the centre are perceived as extreme. The problem, however, is that advocates of such peripheral opinions do not perceive them as extreme and as being on the outside, but rather as being natural, right, self-evident, understandable and so on.

Extreme sports thus understood are not cultivated, sought out and participated in by the majority. They are not the imaginary centres of the general population, or of sports populations. The increasing measure of risk, bordering on hazard, is the factor that drives these movement activities out of the margins of exercise. The increased role played by chance (which is beyond the influence of the individual) is the characteristic measure of hazard. The risk that is dependent on lucky chance can appear too high. That means that the danger of harm and failure, of threat to health and life, is greatly increased in these activities.

It is self-evident, or commonsensical, that such sports offer these experiences at too high a price on occasion, with death or a lasting disability as consequences. In this sense they are truly 'extreme'. We would expect them to be rather marginal in our societies in general and merely a minor constituent of the class of movement activities. But, it can be argued, reality contradicts this common sense. Extreme sports enjoy maximum publicity. They are not on the margins but at the centre of thinking reflection on the topic of sport. Risk sports are not just a matter of fashion. They are not an aberration which will pass away after two or three years or even decades. On the contrary, adventure sports express very clearly and graphically the characteristic of current (postmodern) experience. The crisis of experiencing, the existential frustration, the absence of the reflective meaning of one's own life are but a few examples of this mien. It is the expression of a situation that forces us to think afresh because it offers us meanings which we do not know historically.

The popularity of extreme sports is increasing significantly (witness special journals, TV programmes or web sites from recent years). Their popularity forces us to ask questions not only of a psychological kind, but also relating to cultural studies, sociology and philosophy. How is it that extreme performance and extraordinary experience situations are so attractive for people? What are the fundamental aspects of the challenge situation and whence the motivation to overcome it? What ontological character does the experience in extreme sports have? How can the analysis of extreme sports help the ontological analysis of experience? These are deep and relevant philosophical questions for extreme sportsmen and -women.

Another important moment of postmodern culture and civilization is connected with the idea of 'experience' itself. It speaks to the relation between reality and virtual reality. In another guise it is the relation of one's own experiencing to the taking-over of others' experiences. For example, everybody 'knows' what it is to be freezing in the mountains – but who really goes through it? Everybody gets to see frostbitten feet on TV or in a book – but who lives through it themselves? We can see violent death, killing and war in the media daily so we accept it as a common feature of our lives – but can we really understand the depth of suffering that people experience in such situations just from flat and sensationalist reporting? In the same way the relation between reality and virtual reality is evident in extreme sports: all people watch TV reports, they view web pages, they indulge themselves with 'extreme' and 'cool' images through the use of identifying language or by wearing the 'right' clothing or taking this or that supplement. But the real calling of the challenge and authentic experiencing of adventure activities is, nonetheless, the property of a minority society: a subculture. It is not only an anthropological question but an ontological one as well. If shared social experiences substitute and replace a person's own experience by multimedia, communication means, animation, audiovisual media and so on, we may not be able to distinguish between the real or factual and the virtual. What is real? What engages our being? And what is merely an illusion, a deception of untrue technological modification of appearances, relations, events?

Experience in language

The relation of experience and ontology, however, requires first of all an important terminological note. The word 'experience' may be understood in two ways. First, it may be taken to mean some event that affects or involves a person.

This meaning is expressed in German as *Erlebnis*, in French as *impression*, in old Greek as *eforan*, in Russian as *pe[v]rez[v]ivanije* and in Czech we use the term *prožitek*.[2] And it is this meaning that I will consider in the following part of my presentation. The second meaning of the term 'experience' is some knowledge, skill, wisdom gained through practice in some activity. It is expressed in German as *Erfahrung*, in French *expérience*, in old Greek *empeiria*, respectively *epistémé*, in Russian *ópyt* and in Czech *zkušenost*. Not all languages (including English) apprehend or mark this distinction. Other languages do not observe other aspects of experiencing. For example Slovak and Russian do not distinguish between 'to undergo experience' and 'to survive'. Thus a complex situation emerges when we try to understand this notion in international academic and sporting communities, particularly in a language which is insufficiently nuanced to capture all relevant distinctions with respect to our experience of the world. In spite of this inherent and extreme difficulty, I shall attempt it here.

Why might a philosopher ask about the phenomenon of experience? Because it is a theme that is inordinately emphasized in the postmodern period; it is one of the most frequently used words nowadays. The leisure industry constructs its identity in terms of, and advertises its products on the lines of, 'experience'. The promises about experience made in terms like 'authentic', 'original', 'extreme', 'intensive', 'deep' and so on, intrude into the life of every individual. Extreme sports are a typical example of practical realization of these promises. And paradoxically, at the same time, the truly deep experiences which give meaning to common life wither away. Modern men and women have become hunters of enjoyment and collectors of entertainments and delights which neither lead toward the meaning of life nor toward authentic existence.

Where can we encounter the theory of experience? Psychology takes in the process of consciousness. Experiential education uses the fact that we can learn better in the process of experience more broadly conceived, than through seeing or hearing. On the borderland of psychology, both educational applications and intense theoretical analysis is the theory of optimal experience built on the term 'flow' by Csikszentmihalyi. This theory gives many impulses to psychological understanding of the high popularity of extreme sports. Despite its justly deserved fame, however, it is not especially sympathetic towards the ontological aspects of experience, and so I will merely pass over it here in favour of a more philosophically inclined examination.

Experience in philosophical tradition

Philosophical thinking is always associated with experiencing in some way. One basic example is seen in the fact that thinking is part of a wider stream of experiencing; an individual lives his/her own life in all kinds of modes, while thinking is only one of them. We can see in the history of thinking not only the determination of norms of what is right and wrong in human experiencing, but also in broader ideas at an anthropological level. Thus we may ask, which ways of human experiencing have depth? And how is human life different from other forms of life? Even in these questions it is apparent, however, that we are still missing a strictly ontological evaluation of experience. Experience and experiencing is not an explicit topic of philosophy in antiquity nor the middle ages, nor indeed from the beginning of modern times.

Only the philosophical schools that criticize the one-dimensionality of rationalism take notice of this theme in a more detailed way. Romanticism is among the first. In the late eighteenth and early nineteenth century, Romanticism[3] develops Rousseau's accentuation of emotion and sentiment (which are equal in ratio), in which values and ideals such as heroism, fantasy, imagination and intuition, ardent feeling, passion and spontaneity are emphasized more than in day-to-day reality. Another tradition of philosophical writing might be labelled as 'philosophy of life'[4] which extends the possibilities of cognition for intuition, instinct, direct beholding and so on, and it moves experience into the central point of this thinking. Third, hermeneutical writings[5] are important for an understanding of experience in their interrogation of the concept of understanding, which is different from a 'mere' explanation and description. Every partial understanding, they argue, is already inserted into the framework of pre-understanding. Pre-understanding is not closed. Rather, it is open for permanent deepening and correction of new contents of sense. But it is necessary to look for the connection of sense in a given thing, to take it on its own terms. And it is not possible to pursue this examination from the outside, so to speak. The fundamental tendency of phenomenology (for example in the writings of Husserl) is 'to come back to things themselves', it is to let things (phenomenona) happen as they offer themselves to us. Then consciousness of the things themselves can be achieved by the methods of reduction (in three phases). For Husserl, philosophy means a directly descriptive analysis of experiences. At the same time, he criticizes psychologism, which does not permit the investigation of the senses themselves. The fundamental ontology of Heidegger highlights the problematics of authentic experiencing. He argues that the basic mode of experiencing is care (man/woman first seeks what he/she needs for life). Nevertheless we are able to become conscious of the difference between being and beingness and then between non-authentic existence (to understand myself by way of the things that I commit to) and authentic existence. This mode of understanding is to be contrasted with the use of the same words in advertisements that lure us into various attractions as 'authentic experience'. These mealy-mouthed words have nothing in common with authenticity in Heidegger's writings.

So far it appears that the brief survey of the history of philosophy does not provide us with the ontology of an experience as a way of getting to or at the 'being of the beingness' so to speak (from Heidegger's point of view). This seems still to be missing. Could extreme sports offer us another example that might fruitfully instantiate experience? I am convinced that they can. Before this, however, two further, basic terms, which are necessary to that enterprise, require methodical exploration: 'world' and 'possible worlds'. To these I now turn.

World and possible worlds

The term 'possible world' was introduced to philosophy by Leibniz (1646–1716), who considered possible worlds in connection with theological problems. This world of ours is the best of all possible worlds thanks to a pre-established harmony of monads (elementary, indivisible substances, the simplest entities of world). The term 'possible world', however, is a term of logic and analytic philosophy. I suggest that it is possible to demonstrate also its ontological relevance to and close relationship with experience.

In logic we conceive possible worlds as alternative to the real, actual, world. We imagine the worlds of what could be. We can for example imagine the world in which mountain climbing is an obligatory job for everybody; or a world in which the idea of a ball, and thus the thing itself, does not exist. Equally we might imagine a world in which every football player has four legs. A possible world is different from the actual world in three ways: the same things exist but they have different attributes, qualities, relations (mountain climbing as an obligatory job for all). Or there might be occurrences or beings that are not in the actual world (the football player with four legs). Or, to the contrary, there might exist things or experiences which though we know them now, and which are in the actual world, we might otherwise not know (such as life without [the] idea of a ball[s]). Every such possible world is an alternative of the real world, and there is an infinite number of possible worlds of which only one is real.

Is the category 'possible worlds' not merely a logical possibility, but an onto-logical one, too? I suggest it is. I shall present a consideration concerning the ontological dignity of possible worlds as worlds that could be. Using the criterion of experience, I introduce a device that introduces us to possible worlds and which may determine its ontological reality. As far as I know, no exploration of such an idea has been published in the academic environment of the English language. Some areas of human experiences which are generally respected in the history of culture may help us find some possible way of making sense of this idea of the ontological dignity of possible worlds.

The analysis of mythical rituals reveals a practice of repeating acts of supranatural beings, not merely their imitation, by participants of these rituals. We understand myths as verbal interpretations, but it is possible to experience a reoccurrence of past actions which have taken place between gods and heroes as a way of identifying with them. For example, maenads (female participants in ancient Greek Dionysian rites) were convinced that they were free from typical human limitations, that they were resistant to injury and were able to touch fire without getting burned. Our interpretation of these mythical happenings ought not necessarily to be restricted to the hidden abilities of magicians or sensation-alists. We can use the hypothesis of possible worlds to consider that humans too alter their behaviour and world in ecstatic states and magic ceremonies; we can imagine them changing not only their own abilities but also their attributes of being. In this way a person changes the actual world into another, possible world in which, for example, fire does not burn biotic human tissue, in which unification of the human being is possible in transcendence, in which many counterfactual things happen that would be impossible in the real, actual, world.

Probably every religious complex confesses various worlds which are not commensurate with the earthly world and which are essentially different. 'This' world and 'that' world or 'the other world', sky or various heavens, hells or diverse underworlds, and lower regions, kingdoms of the dead and so on are but the most obvious examples. Many religions explicitly formulate guides into these kingdoms for the dead. These possible worlds may be accepted or refused, they may be protected or satirized. The particular attitude adopted depends on whether one is an apologist or a critical opponent of such dispositions; whether one is, or is not, so to speak, a 'believer'. If these antagonistic testimonies have relevance for our considerations of ontology, we can accept our own authentic experience as a tool of acceptance or non-acceptance of these worlds. We may agree that the employment of rationality is insufficient for the recognition *or* rejection of these hypothesese. Theological constructions are thus established on the same level of rationality as their refusal by atheists. The experience of some strong moment of communication or mystic identification with transcendence is for the experiencing person the inconvertible evidence of recognition of ontological reality of this possible world. This might be analogous to the position of those who experience a religious conversion or a sublime experience on a mountain peak. Authentic experiences afford a certainty rather like this. If somebody has not had such an experience, however, their scepticism towards these possible worlds and their ontological reality appears to them to be reasonable, authorized, even obligatory. Belief or disbelief remains the basic attitude for a majority of people without possibility of verification of this validity by reason or science. The sacrament of the Eucharist (the Lord's supper) entails for Christians the presence of the body and blood of Jesus. To the non-believer it represents only the dish of bread and wine. These interpretations signify completely different worlds, not merely different experiences.

Where is the boundary of different perceptions between believer and sceptic and the experience of the real world? When is a different world to be considered a possible world? Can we experience as ontologically real a world that is at the same time different from this actual one?

The solution to this question is offered in Husserl's category 'horizon'. We have already noted that a concrete separate thing is never alone. The 'horizon' exists within a complex of relations and a number of different interconnections. At the same time every act of thinking takes place within some horizon. The horizon is never closed but it is open and it penetrates other horizons, horizons of other meanings including horizons of possible relations, horizons of virtuality. The summary of these horizons creates the world as contextuality and coherence of connections. The more exact difference between a horizon of all possibilities of the actual world and ontologically different other possible world defines the same category of possible world: the other beingness, absent beingness, different attributes of the same beingness. If anybody experiences some event that appears not to be present in the actual world (such as in the relation of divinity and humanity), we can speak not only about new possibilities of non-experienced actual world, but also of experiences of other worlds, different from the actual world.

Can a philosophical tradition bring some supportive arguments to the hypothesis that we may experience possible worlds, different from the common actual world? We certainly can see some parallels with Plato's world of ideas and in the philosophy of Whitehead with his eternal objects, which are however inherent in real objects. Whitehead even speaks about an 'imaginary world of dreams' with its own space and time. Or perhaps we can employ Popper's idea of three worlds: that is the physical world of direct experience, the psychical world of mental states and perceptions, and the spiritual/cultural world which is a product of the former and in which all human knowledge is generated.

What does 'time' mean?

Try to explain what time is and you run into those problems with which philosophy has been struggling for several centuries already: we all know what time is, but if we want to explain it to anybody else, it is very hard going. How did people think through this topic in the past?

Aristotle analysed time as being related to movement and, further, as being completely independent of the experiencing individual. Movement is uninterrupted in the same way as time, so time is either the same as movement, or some determination of movement. Time becomes measurable, quantified and mechanical by such conceptions, which are undoubtedly useful. The experienced structure of time is, however, distinct from this. It approaches more closely the understanding of St Augustine, who overcomes the interconnection of time with physical categories of movement and space by thinking in three dimensions of time. And when he refers to the fact that time rather 'is not' than 'is' (because the past already is not, the future is not yet, and the present is so slight that the majority of time actually is not at all!), he expands this problematic to include the psychological standpoint: it is the psyche itself that unites these three phases of time. He arrives at the conviction that we measure time in our minds, because we measure the impression that things make on us and which persists even though the primary stimulation has passed. This immediate human topicality (which ties it neither to space nor to any other physical objectivization) is characteristic also of Husserl's conception.

Husserl derides the analysis of time as an objective quantity. Instead he analyses time as consciousness. He argues that we are not able to show time as something objective. Nevertheless, it is possible to search for how we perceive time by rational means. Two moments characterize the present consciousness: retention (the keeping of the past) and protention (the anticipation of the future). The present as a clearly delimited 'now' is made more complicated thereby and attains a complex structure of effluxion and reverberation in continuous action; the continuum of persistency and expectation; the continuous passage of retentions and protentions in a continuous experiencing stream. The stream of continuous change and absolute subjectivity is the phenomenon constitutive of time. Experience has no spatial dimension but time: the present (the absolute now) plays the key role in this thinking. The experiencing stream springs from it. Heidegger thus emphasizes a future that is identified with the openness of possibility. The characteristics of time become a categorical determination of all things experienced by human beings.

Extreme sports and time in experience

With these lengthy but necessary preparatory phenomenological steps we can now consider the central point of this chapter: how an ontology of possible worlds could help the analysis of ontological aspects of experience, and how it could be illustrated by extreme sports. It is evident that one of the basic moments of the structure of experience is time. But it is not physical, uni-directional, linear time. The experience of time is not homogeneous but has a rich structure. It may depend on interest, concern and concentration, or, to the contrary, on feelings of fear and anxiety of the experiencing person.

We live out some events or our lives very quickly while others seem to go very slowly, irrespective of how the clock measures the same section. So we can think about time expanding and contracting in our experience of it. The alterity of time-experience often depends on the age of experiencing people. A small child lives time slower than an old human; an older organism is distinguished by a smaller number of physiological processes and a psychologically smaller number of events. It may depend on bodily temperature: the higher the temperature, the slower is time. It may depend on the speed of one's metabolism; or on the clarity of perception; or it may be influenced by, for instance, mind-altering drugs. It may depend on the quantity of preceding experience or on the novelty of the experienced situation, and so on. The experience of time could depend on the health or illness of the organism; on temperament and the kind of mood one was in.

Notice now, if you will, how the topic of time-relativism in experience is very clear in extreme sport experience. Consider the example of a parachute jump with time extension and compare it with the high rope experience and its time depression. Anybody who is jumping from an aeroplane experiences completely different time coordination in free fall than in everyday situations, e.g. in walking on the pavement. The present time is experienced as if extending and taking over a much wider place than could be objectively true (e.g. by the clock). This fact is very easily demonstrated by beginners and their first jumps. If estimation of the time moment of opening of the parachute is left to them, the time compresses radically (estimates of around half of the time measure span is quite normal). On the contrary, when time is 'expanded' we can see its 'contraction' in experiencing (and in the observation of) a high rope manouevre. The moment when we cross from one tree to another at the height of 10 metres in order to jump towards a horizontal bar halfway across, is experienced as very short. Our full concern, decision-making and delay shorten all time-space in our consciousness, while a much longer time passes for the spectators below.

By what is this different time created? Is it only the first-person estimation of a rigid time span? I am sure that it is not. We cannot speak only about the psychical dimension of time; we must also consider its ontological embeddedness. Wholly changed attributes of beingness point towards different horizons of understanding; point to changes from our common world into other possible worlds. And this projection into a possible world in which time and space coordinates have different dimensions from those they have in the commonly experienced world is noteworthy. Bungee jumping, free-style climbing, high rope courses or the 'ultimate challenge' of all range sports lead us in our experiences into a world with a different horizon of understanding beingness and its meanings. We can see the entrance into other possible worlds by experience, moreover, when we consider other fields of intense experience. One experiences a clarity of time-displaced experience when one is at the top of one's game in sports, in other forms of play (sexual and erotic), and in extreme states of consciousness. This extension raises a number of new possibilities. For example, game and play experiences were notable in previous play research (for example, in the work of Caillois, Fink and Huizinga) where they were conceived of as something not completely real; not right; illusive; apparent; or as mirror reflection of reality. In each of these guises play was understood as something ontologically non-independent. But an ontological conception of possible worlds gives these intense experiences greater support. If sex and eroticism are not described explicitly physiologically and biologically (for example as purely a consequence of genetic inheritance), they are assumed as the private sphere of an individual's life. We can see sex and eroticism as sacredness and sanctity in cultic sacral prostitution, or the mythical *hieros gamos* (holy wedding) in religious systems of antiquity, as magic influence of the productivity of earth. Equally the connection of sexual experience and ontology can be seen in old Indian tantric rituals, too.

The application of the hypothesis of possible worlds into extreme (and other) forces us to concede its significant connection with ontology. Extreme states of consciousness disturb the common understanding of the psycho-physical problem (the so-called mind-body problem). They are described, but they are not explained. Authentic and original experiences place before us questions that demand not merely theoretical explanation, but also challenges to the contemporary scientific paradigm as a whole. Extreme states of consciousness are placed beyond the horizon of so-called 'normal science'. Explication of these experiences may be valuable as an entry into possible worlds that are different from the actual world in their ontological evaluation too. Extreme sports, however, bring us one more motive of experiencing.

Because rationality is a dominant attribute of Western society, its evaluation oppresses emotionality which subsequently and progressively atrophies. What counted as intense human experiences in the past, is considered normal today. Everything is stronger and faster: techno-music, horrors, pornography, drugs – these are typical ways of relaxation in postmodern human life. There is no space for modulation and cool-down, no empty time, no meditation or aesthetic contemplation. The placid aesthetic enjoyment is felt as experience only extraordinarily, while any distraction and excitement are as experienced as normal. The superabundance of stimulation and permanent intensification of self-indulgence of experience into short-term ecstasy is a feature of our postindustrial world that destroys the natural structure of experiencing. This acceleration and intensification of pickup of experiences – without reference to their connection with reality (or virtuality) and ethical embeddedness (in the absence of value-rooting points of view with their emphasis only on their capacity to stimulate) – is a distinct quality of present experience and experiencing. With this way of life, however, there is also a connection to non-authenticity (in Heidegger´s sense) or unnaturalness.

Instead of a conclusion: some questions about meaning

Which meaning(s) can we perceive in extreme sports? Or, more precisely put, by what means could extreme sports bring meaning into our lives? The meaning of life is a category in the history of philosophy which comes up minimally in the reasoning of the ancient Greek Sophists, who were the first we know of to turn their attention from cosmological questions to questions of human being or being human. Questions emerge such as whether it is possible to sense the abstract meaning of life as an independent existence; or, what it is necessary to discover, reveal or acquire? It is also possible, however, to see it in the shape of Plato's idea (or Popper's 'third world') which stands outside of the real world.

We cannot find the meaning of life as something objective, some value or sense valid for all people without difference. On the contrary. Frankl documents, on the basis of experiences and observations from the Nazi concentration camps, that the meaning of life is a category which is thoroughly personal, which belongs to each unique personality or individuality. The meaning of life could be perceived as a constructive work or as a relation to another human being in the form of love. But it is possible to perceive suffering by this prism if we understand it, for example, as a sacrifice.

Which meanings do extreme sports have? What do extreme sports contribute to the meaning of our life? I think we can see in the main their meaning, value and significance at least in the following six points:

1 they saturate the need to obtain extraordinary experiences, to overcome the boundary of normality and to step out from the zone of sureness and security;
2 they warn of the relativity of the perception of given situations as common or adventurous (any measure for the evaluation of situations as dangerous is relative);
3 they put questions to us all about the quality and value of experiences in postmodern time;
4 they document the non-homogeneity of experiencing time and in this way they can contribute to an ontological analysis of experience;
5 they point out ambiguous values and the brittle boundary between life and death (and their reciprocal interconnection); and

6   they increase the value of challenging situations (to accept the challenge has a higher value for the advocate of extreme sports than life without acceptance of this challenge).

It is in the consideration of the very idea of 'experiencing' and other possible worlds that we may also find other evaluations of extreme sports.[6]

Notes

1 Although there is more than one way to understand this: a more accurate account might characterize sport as an effort to achieve maximally, with the goal of a victory by the rules of competition. For all areas of intentional movement activities – including physical education (or more accurately movement education), movement recreation, movement therapy, and movement art – the term movement culture or physical culture is used here.
2 More precisely, there are even two terms in Czech for this meaning, *proz[v]itek* and *záz[v]itek*, but the semantic difference between them is not clear in language.
3 Examples of which I take to be Novalis, the Schlegel brothers, R. W. Emerson, F. E. D. Schleiermacher and F. W. J. Schelling.
4 In writers as disparate as Bergson, Dewey, Dilthey, James and Klages.
5 As represented by Apel, Droysen, Gadamer, Habermas and Ricoeur.
6 This study was prepared within the framework of research MSM 61989221, 'Physical Activity and Inactivity of Inhabitants of the Czech Republic in the Context of Behavioral Changes'.

References

Aristoteles (1946) *Metafysika* (*Metaphysics*), Prague: Jan Laichter.
Augustinus, A. (1990) *Vyznání* (*Confessions*), Prague: Kalich.
Csikszentmihalyi, M. (1996) *O štěstí a smyslu života* (*Flow – the Psychology of Optimal Experience*), Prague: NLN.
Dilthey, W. (1980) *Život a dejinné vedomie* (*Life and Historical Consciousness*), Bratislava: Pravda.
Fink, E. (1993) *Hra jako symbol světa* (*The Game and Play as a Symbol of the World*), Prague: Český spisovatel.
Frankl, V. E. (1994) *Člověk hledá smysl: úvod do logoterapie* (*Human Looking for Meaning: Introduction to Logotherapy*), Prague: Psychoanalytické nakladatelství J. Kocourek.
Frankl, V. E. (1997) *Vůle ke smyslu: vybrané přednášky o logoterapii* (*The Will to Meaning: Selected Papers to Logotherapy*), Brno: Cesta.
Heidegger, M. (1996) *Bytí a čas* (*Being and Time*), Prague: OIKÚMENÉ.
Heidegger, M. (1993) *Konec filosofie a úkol myšlení* (*The End of philosophy and Task of Thinking*), Prague: OIKÚMENÉ.
Husserl, E. (1968) *Karteziánské meditace* (*Cartesian Meditations*), Prague: Svoboda.
Popper, K. R. (1995) *Věčné hledání: intelektuální autobiografie* (*Unended Quest: An Intellectual Autobiography*), Prague: Prostor, Vesmír, OIKÚMENÉ.
Whitehead, A. N. (1989) *Veda a moderný svet* (*Science and Modern World*), Bratislava: Pravda.
Whitehead, A. N. (1970) *Matematika a dobro a jiné eseje* (*Mathematics and the Good and Other Essays*), Prague: Mladá fronta.

12 Kant goes skydiving

Understanding the extreme by way of the sublime[1]

Jesús Ilundáin-Agurruza

Taking off

> If the pain and terror are so modified as not to be actually noxious . . . they are capable of producing delight; not pleasure, but a sort of delightful horror, a sort of tranquility tinged with terror; which, as it belongs to self-preservation, is one of the strongest of all the passions.
>
> T. Burke, *On the Sublime and Beautiful* (Kant, 1951: 118)[2]

Some people jump out of airplanes 13,000 feet above the ground, while others leap off the edge of cliffs or launch themselves down impossibly steep mountains on bikes, and yet others run in front of bulls. The obvious question that arises in most people sane enough to remain spectators is: Why do these people engage in these activities that could cost them life and limb? There are many possible explanations, and the protagonists themselves have multifarious reasons that may or may not agree with what psychologists, sportswriters, and others come up with to elucidate such behavior. Rather than presenting a series of personal disclosures or the psychological analyses of these, I want here to answer the question from a conceptual standpoint that finds a common element to all these experiences. And I want to argue that a specific aesthetic canon handed down from the Enlightenment, the sublime, allows us best to understand what is involved when someone pursues a genuinely dangerous activity that is undertaken as *divertissement*.

At first sight, it seems that the outrageous and untamed phenomenon of the extreme is worlds away from the calm and unruffled demeanor of Enlightenment intellectuals musing on the subject of the sublime. Imagine the following scenario.

The airplane, bouncing around, rapidly gains altitude as it slices through the clouds. Inside the loud cabin there are seven people. Pale faces and fidgety hands embody the tension. Six of them are seasoned skydivers, wearing special skinsuits that will enable them to soar while freefalling at 120 miles an hour – the 'high drag' material on top allows to change less risky. Others, however, will then feel that the goal slips away, the rewards diminish, they do not reach deep levels of satisfaction.

Feinberg maintains that the state should not prevent people from committing risky actions, not even extremely risky actions, simply because they are risky. If the state should prohibit taking such risks, it must be on the ground that the risk is extreme 'and, in respect to its objectively assessable components, manifestly unreasonable to the point of suggesting impaired rationality' (Feinberg, 1986: 103). As I have argued earlier, BASEjumpers are not in this category and BASEjumping should not be prohibited.

Irrational versus unreasonable

Nevertheless some may think that BASEjumpers perform actions that are unreasonable. Some go further and think they are irrational. There is, however, an important distinction to be observed here. People that act irrationally perform actions that are:

> inappropriate means to his own ends, invalid deductions from his own premises, gross departures from his own ideals, or actions based on gross deductions from own premises, gross departures from his own ideals, or actions based on gross delusions and factual distortions.
>
> (Feinberg, 1986: 106)

It would be very hard to argue seriously that BASEjumpers are irrational even if they may seem (or even are) unreasonable. People that are fully normal and rationally competent take unreasonable choices. When we say that choices are unreasonable we do it in a relation to a standard that we think is better. And we indicate that we would not have performed the action had we been in the other person's shoes. In this sense many or even most people think that BASEjumpers act unreasonably. They would not have done the same. Another important aspect here is that unreasonable does not mean unaccountable. We hold unreasonable persons responsible for there actions whereas irrational persons are not fully responsible but 'exculpated'. Irrationality seems to be connected primarily with the person, whereas unreasonableness is connected with single actions. Actions are irrational when they are performed by irrational persons. Unreasonable actions are performed by persons that are usually reasonable and rational. In relation to BASEjumping this means that BASEjumpers are not irrational even though many (or most) people think that BASEjumps are unreasonable actions. If this just means that they would not have done the same themselves, then this is merely a matter of individual preference. It cannot be used as a good reason for moral criticism.

Rational and unreasonable

We should remember that most people can be rational, yet perform actions that are unreasonable:

> Thousands of eminently rational and responsible persons, however, judge that it is not worth the inconvenience to fasten their seat belts in auto-mobiles, or that reducing their risk of getting lung cancer does not justify foregoing the pleasures of cigarette smoking, judgements that I, for one, with all due respect, find unreasonable.
>
> (Feinberg, 1986: 106)

Therefore, we could say that BASEjumpers are rational yet perform actions that are unreasonable. This may however, be too weak. From their own point of view, from the perspective of their deeper life goals, they may thus act reasonably. If the experiences and the performance I seek in life is so intimately connected with BASEjumping that I see no other way to reach my goal or no way that is so satisfying, then it may be reasonable to be involved in BASEjumping.

However, we also have in our intellectual tradition an ideal of what philo-sophers and economists call 'the perfectly rational person', 'practical rationality' or 'economic rationality'. The perfectly rational actor has harmonious goals, weighs them against each other, maximizes his expected utility, chooses means with deliberation, and does not make choices with high costs that make actions unproductive. He does not make impulsive decisions, invest broadly, weigh short term and long term benefits, this year against next year. If such a person does something unreasonable, for instance drinks too much at a party, it is due to an intellectual mistake, a miscalculation.

In reality, however, we have individuals that are very far from such an ideal. They are not prudent and do not like long-term planning. They think the prudent life is boring. Feinberg says:

> Imprudence may not pay off in the long run, and impulsive adventurers and gamblers may be losers in the end, but they do not always or necessarily have regrets. Hangovers may be painful and set back one's efforts, but careful niggling prudence is dull and unappealing. Better the life of spontaneity, impulse, excitement, and risk, even if it be short, and even if the future self must bear the costs.
>
> (Feinberg, 1986: 109)

Feinberg thinks that such adventurers should not be denied the possibility to lead the type of life they want by saying that their preferences are not voluntary and not in the person's own, deep interest and so on. Even worse would be to admit that the person's preferences were genuine but not in accordance with prudence and the idea of a rational life project. That would mean not respecting autonomy and the right of people to lead the lives they want.

Feinberg made the now classic distinction between hard and soft paternalism. It is not clear that the soft version is paternalistic at all. It is close to Feinberg's own views and implies that 'the state has the right to prevent self-regarding harmful conduct (so far it *looks* "paternalistic") *when but only when* the conduct is substantially nonvoluntary, or when temporary intervention is necessary to establish whether it is voluntary or not!' (Feinberg, 1986: 12).

Hard paternalism, on the other hand, means forcing people who are irrational or unreasonable in their actions. Feinberg rejects hard paternalism. He thinks instead that we should open up the moral space to the romantic and irrational in people. We are too much governed by the ideal of 'economic man'. If we can force people to become rational that is ethically a much bigger problem than allowing or enabling people to engage in actions that are irrational or imprudent. Feinberg sees rationality as did Hume and Rawls: rationality is related to choices of means to reach our goals and realize our preferences. But there is not only one way, but a variety of ways and means through which we can reach our goals. Different sets of life plans and lifelines can be developed. Some of our life goals are based on deep preferences tied to genetic makeup, early experiences, relationships to special persons and so on. We should accept diversity both in life goals and also in ways to reach our goals:

> Some people quite naturally prefer adventure and risk to tranquillity and security, spontaneity to deliberation, turbulent passions to safety. Instead of being ostracized as 'not rational', these givens should become part of the test for the rationality of subsequent wants that must cohere with them.
> (Feinberg, 1986: 111)

This means that a person who wants to live her life in strong colours must be judged according to that. For this person it is rational and reasonable to choose actions that cohere with these deep preferences and goals. This would lead to an acceptance of BASEjumping as a possible life project, a goal in a life that needs BASEjumping for fulfilment.

Concluding remarks

I started by asking whether risk sports could be valuable, whether they are morally acceptable or whether some of them should be prohibited by law. I used BASEjumping as a test case since it is one of the most extreme and risky sports. In order to answer the questions I presented some of the intuitive arguments that are most often used in the debate for and against BASEjumping. I then went on to discuss the more developed and systematic views of Sen (1986) and Feinberg (1986) on the right to take risks.

My conclusion is that BASEjumping should not be prohibited by law, as is the case now in many places. I think that people who BASEjump are not irrational. They need not be protected against themselves. There is no need to interfere in a paternalistic way. I also think that BASEjumping can be morally accepted

provided the jumpers behave in a responsible manner. This means that the right
to jump must be balanced against the interests of their families, friends, rescue
personnel and so on. I think Sen's idea of goal rights makes sense here. BASE-
jumping can be morally accepted provided the jumpers are aware of other
responsibilities they have in their lives. This means that BASEjumping as such is
not to be placed in the negative part of the moral space of figure 1. BASEjumping
may, depending upon circumstances, be among the adiafora, in some cases in the
negative space, but it can also represent important and worthwhile values in
the lives of BASEjumpers. BASEjumping may for some people be an important
part of a life project. It may be an important way to realize deeper life goals. Or
rather it is a specification of the kinds of ends they pursue at the deepest level of
meaningfulness for them.

   This positive evaluation does not mean that the problems are dispelled.
We have seen that even if many jumpers are resourceful and responsible people
there are also selfish and cynical jumpers with a big narcissistic ego. The jumpers
need to be aware of their responsibilities towards families and friends. There are
problems related to risks and costs of rescue operations that need to be provided
for through careful arrangements. But these are problems that can be solved
in various ways and they do not as such stop BASEjumping from being an
acceptable and even valuable activity.

Note

1 BASE is an acronym for the four categories of fixed objects BASE jumpers launch from
   – Buildings, Antennas, Spans (bridges) and Earth (cliffs). (See www.baseclimb.com/
   BASEjumping.htm.)

References

Baseclimb (2006) available online at http//www.baseclimb.com/BASE_history.htm
   (accessed 31 October 2006).
Beck, U. (1992) *Risk Society. Towards a New Modernity*, London: Sage Publications.
Bjørgen, T. (1999) 'Holdninger blant basehoppere' ('Attitudes among BASEjumpers'),
   available online at http://www.brv.no/sikkerhet-artikkel.asp?id=177 (accessed 31
   October 2006).
Cashmore, E. (2000) *Making Sense of Sports*, 3rd edn, London and New York: Routledge.
Feinberg, J. (1986) *Harm to Self* (*The Moral Limits of Criminal Law*, vol. 3), New York and
   Oxford: Oxford University Press.
Giddens, A. (1990) *The Consequences of Modernity*, Stanford, CA: Stanford University
   Press.
Gomà-i-Freixanet, M. (2001) 'Prosocial and Antisocial Aspects of Personality in Women:
   A Replication Study', *Personality and Individual Differences*, 30, 1401–11.
Jakeman, S. (1992) *Groundrush*, London: Jonathan Cape.
Lupton, D. (1999) *Risk*, London and New York: Routledge.
Mæland, S. (2002) *B.A.S.E. En studie i samtidskultur. Ekstremt friluftsliv. Eksistensielle
   dilemmaer. Sublime opplevelser* (*B.A.S.E. A study in contemporary culture. Extreme*

outdoor life, existential dilemmas, sublime experiences, Master thesis), Hovedfagsoppgave, Bø: Høgskolen i Telemark.

O'Connell, N. (1993) *Beyond Risk. Conversations with Climbers*, Seattle, OR: The Mountaineers.

Rinehart, R. E. (2000) 'Arriving Sport: Alternatives to Formal Sport', in J. Coakley and E. Dunning (eds.) *Handbook of Sport Studies*, London: Sage Publications.

Sen, A. (1986) 'The Right to Take Personal Risks', in D. MacLean (ed.) *Values at Risk*, Totowa, NJ: Rowman & Allanheld, pp. 155–70.

Yates, F. and Stone, E. R. (1992) 'The Risk Construct', in F. Yates (ed.) *Risk-Taking Behavior*, Chichester: John Wiley & Sons.

14 Walking the edge

Verner Møller

Death awaits us. Patiently. It is in no hurry. But time rushes on. We get older. 'You'll soon be more than seventeen,' sang the popular Danish soft pop singer, Annette Klingenberg, when as a 15-year-old I lay sunbathing on the lawn at my parents' summer house. That was in 1977. The song was disconcerting then. It is no less disconcerting today, when it seems only a moment ago that Klingenberg was in the top ten. My birth certificate tells a different story. Fortunately the song is scarcely ever heard any more – especially if you refrain from listening to the Danish radio programme *giro 413*, which on Sunday afternoons plays listeners' requests, evergreen selections for the older audience, and more than anything else provides a reminder of the proximity of death.

In any event, the song was right. We 'young ones' – to refer even further back to the Cliff Richard song that was all the rage when I was born – who were just embarking on our youth and to whom the song was apparently addressed, did indeed soon pass the seventeen mark. One of my friends, however, made seventeen but no more. On a ferry crossing with some friends, he tried to see if he could walk tightrope along the rail. He could not. He fell overboard, disappeared into the darkness and ended his all too young life in the freezing waters. Later they found him washed up on the shore of a foreign country. Rumour had it at the time that his attempt was motivated by something as prosaic as a bet about a crate of beer. This appears to be too simple an explanation. The bet may have been the immediate cause. And the effects of a couple of drinks may have paved the way by muffling the concern he must have felt about the danger. But it is not credible that the actual cause should have been the prospect of winning a crate of beer on the ferry. The discrepancy between the prize and the risk taken is too great for that to be the case. And even though some amount of alcohol had been drunk beforehand, there is no reason to believe that he was drunk to the point of not being aware of the risk he was running. Inebriation may have been the reason for the attempt ending in disaster, but it can scarcely have been the reason for the attempt having been made. The motive must have been something else, something that can be called *risk attraction*. This fits in with the picture I have of my friend. He loved wind-surfing and got high on the challenge presented by seriously big waves. Nothing seemed too wild for him, until the day when wildness, daredevilry and water joined forces to rob him of his life. This curious, fascinating and at times fatal risk attraction is the subject of the present article.

Train-surfing and other risks

The French sociologist David LeBreton (1991) draws attention to an arresting article published in the *Libération* newspaper on 20 January 1988. The article tells the story of young 15- to 20-year-olds who 'surf' on the roofs of overcrowded trains travelling between Rio de Janeiro and the residential areas of the city's suburbs. The train races along at about 50 m.p.h. The surfers on the roof struggle to keep their balance and avoid falling off while at the same time evading bridges and high-voltage cables. Of course we think about the danger of accidents, recounts one of the surfers interviewed, but in the first instance we climb onto the roof because there is no room inside the train. At the beginning people lie down flat on their stomachs and hold on tight. But that gets boring after a while, so they sit up and then later try to stand up. When the wind thrusts right in your face and you have to lean forward and fight the wind, then the game is on for real. It gives you a special sort of feeling of being high. There are even some of them who wait to do their train-surfing until after dark, so they can hardly see anything and have to trust their instinct. This increases the risk, of course, but then it's that much more exciting.

Most branches of sport involve some element of risk. If you play badminton, there is an increased risk of snapping your Achilles tendon. In soccer there is the risk of cruciate ligament damage and fractures. If you ride, there is the risk of falling off the horse and breaking your back. To enumerate the sports that involve a particular risk of one kind or another could be a lengthy exercise. But what is common to the majority of sports is that the risk element is not a significant part of the attraction. If people play football or take part in competitive cycling, then they show themselves to be prepared to take a risk. They are willing to run the risk that is necessary for them to win. They will slide tackle or whiz through hairpin bends without using their brakes any more than is absolutely necessary. Sometimes it happens that a football player enters a tackle too late or at the wrong angle. Sometimes the cyclist underestimates the sharpness of a bend and falls off. This can result in serious injury. These are risks that people have to be willing to take, for otherwise they cannot take part. But once the game has started, the risk is of no importance.

Train-surfing as a mirror of society

With train-surfing it is a different story. Here we have one activity in an ever-lengthening list of unorganised sporting activities in which the element of risk plays a central part. If I consider so marginal a phenomenon in the field of extreme sports as Brazilian train-surfing worth drawing attention to, it is because in a very precise manner it paints a picture of modern conditions for survival, which, taken as a whole, occasion the growth of forms of activities that seem to defy common sense. The newly industrialised Brazil, South America's super-power, is a country of extreme contrasts. There is enormous wealth, and there is abysmal poverty. It is like looking at the remarkable duality of the modern Western welfare state through a magnifying glass.

In general, established welfare states are characterised by a hitherto unknown degree of security, but through the mesh of the safety net threats can still be glimpsed. It is certainly the case that never before in history have so many people been so free of hazards as they are now – in terms of their finances, their health and their military security. This can be ascertained in concrete terms from aggregate life salaries, from average life expectancies and from the actual absence of any military threat to the Western world. We can thank the capitalist economy and market forces that things have developed this way. But capitalism's overall success does not come without a price tag. This is something we can easily forget in our exhilaration at the manifest elimination of the West's image of the enemy, the so-called 'evil empires' of the great Communist powers, the Soviet Union and China, whose attempts at planned economies could not measure up to the development of capitalist countries. In the wake of the dissolution of the Soviet Union, the various erstwhile members of that Union are now experimenting with market economies on the Western model, just as China is doing. And those countries that have the chance to amalgamate entirely with the West are doing all they can to ensure that this happens as quickly as possible. This can be seen from the developmental process of the European Union.

Those countries that have been late in releasing market forces are currently paying a high price for their investment in a better future. Large swathes of the population are being impoverished. The lesson being learned by new market-oriented countries is that the success of capitalism is based on mutual competition between members of their society. And in a competitive society there will always be winners and losers. In older welfare states there are attempts to mitigate or camouflage this factor with the help of various welfare arrangements. Inequality and the human costs are nevertheless unmistakeable. Such costs can be seen not only in the queues at benefits offices and outside the department of unemployment. They are also evident on park benches and in soup kitchens, in the form of alcoholism, homelessness and hunger.

The outcasts of society, those on benefit, the alcoholics, the homeless and so on, are seen as a burden on society. They are, however, by no means as useless as we might be led to believe. For they serve as a constant reminder of the dangers we run, if we do not submit to the social imperative to get into harness and follow the herd. They stand as living testaments to the risk of total fiasco that haunts us despite the abundance of opportunities for success, for earning money and saving for retirement that are available in wealthy societies to normally endowed normal individuals, who – despite so much modern talk of flexibility and adaptability – possess what remains the most significant of qualifications, namely the ability to conform and to do their duty.

Modern welfare states are like trains set on rails. They career along, full steam ahead, up hill and down dale. Any influence the individual might have on its direction is by and large negligible. But nevertheless each of us has to make sure we are on board. The alternative – to be left behind on the platform – holds little attraction. This is the drama that the train-surfers are enacting.

The surfers want to be part of the roadshow. They hold on for dear life. But there is no room in the carriages, so they climb up onto the roof. Here they find a place in obscurity, at the periphery of good society. They travel back and forth on schedule but without ever coming in from the cold. In the beginning it is both frightening and challenging, but in the long run it is felt to be insufficient, disheartening, boring. The action of sitting up and then standing on one's own two feet is essentially human. It implies the development of skills, the achievement of an ever greater degree of command and control. Risk attraction does indeed seem to relate to the hunt for ever greater experience of control and command. This leads the risk-taker to seek out the field of tension between challenge and skill. The attraction does not lie in a complete command of the situation, for total command is synonymous with the elimination of the challenge as challenge. The area over which we possess complete control gives us no sense of control. This is why the field of tension between the ability to control and the risk of fiasco and complete helplessness holds the real attraction. *The fear is essential.*

The necessity of fear

The growth in activities in which the element of risk plays a central role indicates at one and the same time surplus and deficit. Unlike train-surfing, many of these activities demand considerable resources. Adventure tourism, mountaineering and mountain-climbing, extreme ski sports, deep-sea diving and similar activities require capital. Such activities are for people of substance. Without prosperity, without surplus, the adventure market could not be cultivated. There must, however, also be another precondition present, namely a deficit in the form of a need.

Now we must not go round thinking that people have been born with a need to risk their lives by, for example, skiing in unknown terrain down almost vertical cliffs. But there are grounds for believing that risk activities do nevertheless answer a fundamental need, namely the need to be in control. As it happens this need is something that the philosopher Friedrich Nietzsche identified when he wrote:

> Physicians should think twice before positioning the drive for self-preservation as the cardinal drive of an organic being. Above all, a living thing wants to *discharge* its strength – life itself is will to power –: self-preservation is only one of the indirect and most frequent *consequences* of this.

> (Nietzsche, 2002: 15)

The welfare state has been constructed with a view to providing security for those members of society who are not able to achieve power over their lives, yet it is not in a position to satisfy the individual's need to feel that he has such power. On the contrary, there is a tendency for it to have the opposite effect, as well as having a negative influence on those who do in reality possess such power. For the welfare state consolidates and regulates power structures in such a way that power remains unchallenged, but also so that, for those who do have power over their lives, the very experience of power disappears. For the welfare state takes power over – and for – its citizens. And it is *essentially* a guardian state. Notwithstanding all its advantages, its effect is to deprive citizens of self-determination. It creates tutelage.

The consequence of the historically high security that living in a welfare state brings with it is that it becomes particularly difficult to become adult in a substantive sense of the word. The unemployed have a marked sense of being treated as children, and many lose their self-respect when, in order not to lose their 'pocket money', they allow themselves to be shepherded round in various forms of job training, retraining and other well-meant schemes for 'activation'. Making the unemployed into 'clients' (along with its resultant infantilisation) masks the general incapacitation and powerlessness of the general public. But there are those who are simply not able to wrap themselves up in the illusion that they have power over their lives, or to be satisfied with having power they cannot feel because in reality there is no opposition to it. Whether they have power or not, they perceive disempowerment as a condition of living within the framework of the welfare state and therefore seek out other areas in which to exercise mastery. For the most part they follow their studies or do their jobs, living with the best of prospects, but they nevertheless experience the security of the welfare state as something that oppresses – even depresses – them. Security places them in a state of restlessness, which they counter by seeking out risk (Apter, 1992).

When, therefore, they act as though they had lost their mind, what they are doing is actually trying to keep their mind healthy. This means that what appears as madness in risk activities is, in reality, the development of a form of sense that is other than common sense. Extreme sports in other words function as mental health activities for dealing with the problems created by the welfare state – namely that in reality it makes fear homeless. This homeless fear, transformed in turn to angst, imposes itself on everything both large and small. It is in the homelessness of fear that we can find the causes for anxiety and for exaggerated concerns about such phenomena as immigration, pollution, terrorism, salmonella, mad cow disease, the closure of our local hospital and so on. In line with this train of thought the sociologist Zygmunt Bauman writes:

> One of the foremost services that the underclass renders to the present-day affluent society is the sucking in of the fears and anxieties no longer drained by a potent enemy outside. The underclass is the enemy inside the walls, destined to replace the external enemy as a drug crucial to collective sanity; a safety valve for collective tensions born of individual insecurity.
>
> (Bauman, 1998: 72)

If people are not to be plagued by angst, there must be something concrete to fear. What Bauman is pointing to is fear as an inescapable condition of human existence. The fundamental form of fear manifests itself in relation to death. If only a minority of people are plagued by persistent fear of death, it is because most people fill out their time with tasks of various kinds which can occupy their concerns in a concrete way. Busyness keeps fear at bay. On the other hand fear can invade at moments when our busyness is suddenly felt to be meaningless, or when our tasks disappear and life all at once seems senseless or purposeless (retirement with its loss of focus and the less well-observed networks of meaning and identity. It is important to be on the go. However, as I have said, not everyone manages to be satisfied with functioning smoothly as a little cog in a large social machine. For them the tattered vision of the underclass is not sufficient to manacle fear. They are looking for something more concrete to relate to (Opaschowski, 2000). Whether it is standing on the roof of a speeding train, climbing high up on a tricky cliff face, whizzing down steep mountainsides or free-diving deep down towards the ocean floor, the fear is real. Risk demands total concentration. All else has to be locked out – forgotten. You have to be one with the situation, surrender to it, fuse with it. The consequence is momentary self-forgetting. And this is yet another significant aspect of the attraction of extreme sport.

Relation to self and self-forgetting

When practitioners are asked to explain why they are attracted by high-risk activities, as a rule they stress *the attraction of the high* as an important element. Typical is the statement by the Danish mountain-climber Lars Gundersen, prior to his joining the expedition to climb Tibet's 8,046 metre high Shisha Pangma in the spring of 1998:

> I am not driven by a death wish. I wouldn't want to risk my little finger for a mountain. I am, of course, driven by the danger, survival, and by the adrenalin kick it gives. And by a whole lot more, too, that I can't explain . . . I get grabbed by that vertical world. As a climber and a mountaineer you are always fighting with your self. Can you do *that* move on the cliff-face or can't you? Will you fall, or won't you? All the time you have to make decisions where there is only an either-or. All the time you want to push yourself further. You get a thrill out of the experience of arranging and carrying out expeditions. With greater levels of difficulty and higher mountains.
>
> (Halbirk, 1998: 12)

Gundersen declares himself for life, not for death. He will not risk so much as a little finger to achieve the goal he sets for himself, he says. And yet he invests everything to get there. He knows that what he does often throws up situations that involve an ultimate either-or. He trusts blindly in *either*, but pushes himself further and further out towards *or*. It is paradoxical but not beyond the bounds of understanding. For although putting your life at risk to reach the top of a mountain more than 8 kilometres high just to start your descent a few moments later looks like madness to the outsider, the act increases the life intensity of the members of the expedition. Not to do it would for them be tantamount to letting their life go to waste. To live life in its daily grind without experiencing the kick of moving out of the groove and feeling the pull of the edge is regarded as grey and boring (Csikszentmihalyi, 1975). It is like parking life on the forecourt of death, which is not dangerous but provokes just as much anxiety. For in wasting time, in the emptiness of being, we are thrown back upon ourselves. It is reminiscent of the nightmare that many lonely people find themselves in and which they placate by using tranquillisers and other mind-altering substances. Human beings are presumably the only living beings that – for better or for worse – stand in a relationship with themselves. We are perhaps equal to the animals in experiencing fear. But anxiety – like joy – has our relationship to ourselves as its precondition, and in this we are probably unique. As human beings we have to live with our awareness of ourselves and of our mortality. Human existence is in other words a burden, but for that reason it is also weighty.

In her novel *All Men are Mortal* (1992), the French writer and philosopher Simone de Beauvoir gives a convincing portrayal of the unbearable sense of the meaninglessness of being that plagues the man who cannot die despite the fact that the years pass across his body without leaving a trace. The point elaborated by Beauvoir is that in the light of eternity even the most colourful movements – wars, conquests, voyages of discovery and romances – are inert. And inertia increases the weight of being. It increases attention on the relationship with self and in the end becomes unbearably heavy. It is precisely for this reason that the human animal sets itself in motion; draws up projects and plans. The activities can have any number of aims, but at the deepest level their aim is one and the same: to break inertia and distract attention from the weight of being.

In the welfare state, where the struggle for survival has been suspended, the workplace has become a place of play, with the single difference that the game played here is usually trivial. Business people and investors may think that it is exciting to invest energy and money in risky projects and can find meaning in making businesses flourish. But if it doesn't work, then it is merely tiresome, not fatal. It is not essentially different from losing at sport. It is not deadly serious. Those who involve themselves in it, whether it be sport or work, take it seriously, of course, in the same way that children take their games seriously and allow themselves to be immersed in them. But there are apparently more and more people who do not allow themselves to be satisfied with the fake seriousness of sport or the world of business. To achieve the desired state of self-forgetting and fullness of being they have to seek out tasks with a different and concrete seriousness. Gundersen says this very precisely. It is the danger, *survival*, that drives him on. In other words he is looking for the seriousness of death. Survival is not essential *per se*. It only becomes essential when life is laid on the line. The thrilling experience of arranging and carrying out an expedition is more important than survival precisely because of its seriousness.

Fear of death – a driving force?

Seriousness ties attention to the situation in the moment. The greater the challenge, the greater the need for the concentration of focus. In the most difficult moments, when survival demands complete alertness and concentration, our relation to ourselves is erased, and this can give rise to ecstatic experiences of being fused with the situation and of being at one with everything. The positive outcome is a sense of invulnerability and omnipotence. This feeling, however, fades after a while, and this then stimulates the desire to take new risks. The German psychoanalyst Horst E. Richter sees no strength behind this form of challenge to death:

> There are an endless number of small adventures and athletic works of art, whose stimulation of the nerves is nothing other than a concealed challenge to death. In showing again and again that you can emerge unscathed from dangerous situations which you have stage-managed yourself, you can continue to believe that there is no place and no time in which you will perish. But behind all these exploits of derring-do, anxiety persists and has to be pacified with ever more novel over-compensatory ventures. In a way the 'self-conquest' which these small heroes boast of and which they are admired for is essentially no conquest of what threatens them in the innermost part of their Self. It is precisely because they cannot overcome the real inner fear of weakness and mortality that they hurl themselves at deserts, oceans, mountains – or at other greater or smaller *external* objects of fear. *A demonstration of contempt for death is, therefore, as a rule only an over-compensation for the opposite, namely a powerful fear of dying.*
>
> (Richter, 1980: 158, trans. John Mason, emphasis added)

There can scarcely be any doubt that Richter is onto something when he describes risk activities as a way of relating to existential angst. But his diagnosis of the phenomenon shows signs of a general cultural critique, which renders his argument unbalanced. It is clearly correct to say that death as a central feature of the human condition is taken up and worked as a theme when people voluntarily seek out potentially lethal situations. On the other hand it is far from certain that those people who seek out danger are in reality psychologically more fragile and fearful than people are in general. We cannot, of course, reject the possibility that some people are motivated to seek out dangerous situations as a form of self-therapy for an excessive fear of death, but that this should be the general case is unthinkable. If seeking out risk is a mechanism for displacement, then it is simply one among many. As I have said, human beings are constantly proposing plans and projects to keep themselves in motion and in that way keep death at a safe distance. It is not a logical conclusion to say that because high-risk activities are by nature extreme their practitioners' fear of death is likewise extreme. Furthermore, since we are not dealing here primarily with bungee-jumping or fairground attractions – or in other words with activities in which the risk is not real but is simply experienced as such – the idea of a particularly powerful fear of death as a concealed motive seems not only paradoxical but also problematic in the extreme. Nor is it the case that people with a particularly pronounced claustrophobia time and again lock themselves in small spaces. To arrive at a more satisfactory explanation of risk attraction there seems to be good reason to leave Richter's negative explanatory framework behind.

Being familiar with death

A prominent feature of the development of Western culture is that it has moved from an almost familiar intimacy with death in the Middle Ages to the denial of it in our own time (Ariès, 1975). Attempts to repress it have, however, not succeeded in effecting its disappearance. Making it into a taboo has on the contrary resulted in people in Western cultures having a far more problematic relation to death.

Considering the general and dogged denial of the reality of death, taking it up as a theme in high-risk activities can be regarded as a sacrilegious act that transgresses social boundaries. But putting your life at risk by throwing yourself into activities that entertain or even invite it is a way of bringing death back into life. At particular moments it is desperately frightening. This is when you experience your adrenalin kick. As time passes, this kick is reduced in strength. You become familiar with the danger and have to dare to take a step even closer to the edge in order to feel that ecstatic high. The kick comes as a rule at moments which practitioners term *close calls*, when you are on the point of losing or do actually lose control, but nevertheless manage to save yourself. In these situations death comes close, and this gives it a degree of familiarity that makes it less frightening.

The formidable Italian free-diver Umberto Pelizzari recounts, in an interview written up in the Danish newspaper *Politiken*, that he places considerable emphasis on safety when he practises his sport. Like the mountaineer Lars Gundersen, he is not driven by any death-wish. Nevertheless he runs a colossal risk. To go down to depths of more than 100 metres – even with air canisters on your back – is, according to the chairman of the Danish Diving Sports Association, Karl Gunnar Gregersen, lethally dangerous (Vestergaard, 2000). Pelizzari goes even further down without air and holds the free-diving record of 150 metres. When he dives, he stakes his life, but that does not concern him. When he is down in the darkness, he experiences an intense feeling of freedom and stillness, he says in the article, indicating its attraction for him: 'With each dive I am presented with the choice of remaining down there or swimming up again. But I have no longing for death. Not in the least' (ibid.). Pelizzari has no wish to die, but on the other hand his lack of fear for death shines through. He seems to have achieved serenity, as though his high-risk sport has helped him to arrive at a relaxed relationship to his mortality. Pelazzari seems then to be a living contradiction of Richter's diagnosis of increasing risk behaviour.

We get the same impression from the experienced New Zealand mountaineer Rob Hall, by reading Jon Krakauer's account of the tragedy on Mount Everest in

1996. Hall was the leader and chief guide on the Adventure Consultants' expedition, which Krakauer was on. As Krakauer describes him, Hall was a calm, well-balanced and competent leader with a considerable feeling of responsibility for the clients whom he had undertaken to guide up the world's highest mountain. Hall had devoted his life to climbing. Since he was nineteen he had carried out a large number of difficult climbs. In order to finance these costly expeditions he entered into sponsorship agreements. This alliance was fine for a time. His sponsors got media exposure, and Hall got to climb mountains. But he could see that, if there was to be continued interest in his expeditions, then he was obliged to plan ever more spectacular projects, and he understood that sooner or later he would get too close to the edge – and be found wanting. To avoid that, he went in for the cultivated market for guided expeditions, where clients with dreams of being mountaineers took care of the financing. It was one of these expeditions that went wrong in 1996, when two of his clients, one of his guides and he himself died. With his experience he could certainly have saved his own life, if he had not stayed with one of his clients, Doug Hansen, who had run out of oxygen, and whose fate he must have known was sealed before he chose to seal his own. At a point when the situation is critical and the time has come to make the crucial decision to stay or to go down, Hall is in radio contact with Guy Cotter, one of Hall's old friends. Cotter, himself a mountaineer, is clear about the seriousness of the situation and urgently presses Hall to go down. But Hall rejects his advice. He said that he could easily come down himself, but not with Hansen, and he would simply not consider going down without him. Despite a number of requests, he chose to remain up there. Twenty-four hours later, when he has radio contact for the last time, his own situation is hopeless, and he bids his final farewell to his wife, Jan Arnold, via satellite telephone. Krakauer records the following from the conversation which Hall initiates:

> 'Hi, my sweetheart. I hope you're tucked up in a nice warm bed. How are you doing?' 'I can't tell you how much I am thinking about you!' Arnold replied. 'You sound so much better than I expected . . . Are you warm, my darling?' 'In the context of the altitude, the setting, I am reasonably comfortable,' Hall answered, doing his best not to alarm her. 'How are your feet?' 'I haven't taken my boots off to check, but I think I may have a bit of frostbite . . .' 'I'm looking forward to making you completely better when you come home,' Arnold said. 'I just know you're going to be rescued. Don't feel you're alone. I'm sending all my positive energy your way!' Before signing off, Hall told his wife, 'I love you. Sleep well, my sweetheart. Please don't worry too much.'
> (Krakauer, 1997: 307)

Neither Hall's behaviour in this extremely critical situation nor his final conversation with his wife shows the least sign of any fear of death. He is surprisingly calm. It is as though he has become so familiar with danger through his career as a mountaineer that, when danger becomes fatal, he is able to look it in the eyes with peace of mind. Within the framework of a Western mode of thinking, Hall's apparent serenity and preparedness seem foreign. We will tend to look for explanations for the calm and composure shown in his farewell to his wife on the telephone, finding them in his exhaustion, or in the doziness and lack of clarity that result from lack of oxygen. As Westerners we have difficulty in believing it possible to look death in the face with complete peace of mind. For a Buddhist, however, this is not a foreign thought. In fact, the ideal in Buddhist thinking is to be in a position not only to reconcile oneself to death but to rejoice in it. For Buddhists it is senseless to push death away, since they regard life and death as a complete whole. Death is a mirror in which the meaning of life is reflected. The completeness of life and death are presented in *The Tibetan Book of Living and Dying* as a series of constantly changing states of transition, the so-called *bardos*. A *bardo* can be compared with the moment when we approach the edge of an abyss, and the greatest and most meaningful of these moments is the moment of death (Rinpoche, 2002). Being in a position to overcome the fear of death is seen in Buddhism as the crucial precondition for mastering life. The way to it is, as a rule, through meditation. One branch of Buddhism, however, presents us with an exception to this rule. In Dhayna Buddhism, which is called Zen in Japan, it is immediate experience that is stressed. In his book *Zen in the Art of Archery*, the German writer Eugen Herrigel describes how over a period of six years he was instructed in the art of archery by one of the art's great Zen masters. Herrigel's account is deeply mystical. Strictly speaking it is beyond the power of description. I will therefore make no attempt to give a full account of it here, but simply say that what Herrigel learns is that his will to do stands in the way of his ability to do. He has, therefore, to practise being without worrying, but on another plane than a beginner typically does. It is possible to start something without worrying, because we know nothing of the problems involved, but then, as we meet them, we usually start to worry about whether we are up to the task. Instruction in Zen involves guiding the student on to a higher stage of unconcern and thereby to mastery. To underline what is involved, Herrigel (1995: 103) describes the Samurai's attitude to life:

> Like the beginner the swordmaster is fearless, but, unlike him, he grows daily less and less accessible to fear. Years of unceasing meditation have taught him that life and death are at bottom the same and belong to the same stratum of fact. He no longer knows what fear of life and terror of death are. He lives – and this is thoroughly characteristic of Zen – happily enough in the world, but ready at any time to quit it without being in the least disturbed by the thought of death. It is not for nothing that the samurai have chosen for their truest symbol the fragile cherry blossom. Like a petal dropping in the morning sunlight and floating serenely to earth, so much the fearless detach [sic] himself from life, silent and inwardly unmoved.
>
> (Herrigel, 1979: 103)

The attitude presented here is not unlike that which we saw shining through the words of Hall, Pellizzari and other first-class practitioners of extreme sports. Not every extreme alpinist, surfer – or BASEjumper for that matter – is, of course, a fearless master. What those who stress the kick factor as a significant attraction in these sports reveal is that they have not attained the point beyond fear, despite showing themselves braver than most people. At the same time it cannot be denied that one unvoiced motive for seeking out danger is an underlying sense that the kick offers a way to find meaning of another depth than that which is to be found in a secure existence as productive member of society in the comforting framework of the welfare state. At any rate the welfare state provides us with no protection against death; nor is it in a position to provide us with a meaning for our lives. Meaning is something we have to find – in time – and it is only momentary, the merest twinkling of an eye. The truth of this is what my friend, in a moment of overconfidence, experienced as he fell overboard and was washed up on the shores of a foreign land.

References

Apter, M. (1992) *The Dangerous Edge. The Psychology of Excitement*, New York: The Free Press.

Ariès, P. (1975) *Western Attitudes toward Death: From the Middle Ages to the Present*, Baltimore, MD: Johns Hopkins University Press.

Bauman, Z. (1998) *Work, Consumerism, and the New Poor*, Buckingham, PA: Open University Press.

Beauvoir, S. de (1992) *All Men are Mortal*, New York: W.W. Norton and Company.

Csikszentmihalyi, M. (1975) *Beyond Boredom and Anxiety – The Experience of Play in Work and Games*, San Francisco, CA: Jossey-Bass.

Halbirk, V. (1998) 'Det gælder jo om at overleve' (Survival is the Most Important Thing), *Aktuelt*, Copenhagen, 10 February.

Herrigel, E. (1979) *Zen in the Art of Archery*, London: Routledge and Kegan Paul.

Krakauer, J. (1997) *Into Thin Air*, New York: Doubleday.

LeBreton, D. (1991) *Passion du Risque*, Paris: Éditions Métailié.

Nietzsche, F. (2002) *Beyond Good and Evil*, Cambridge: Cambridge University Press.

Opaschowski, H.W. (2000) *Xtrem – Der Kalkulierte Wahnsinn. Extremsport als Zeitphänomen*, Hamburg: Germa Press.

Richter, H. E. (1980) *Gudskomplekset* (*The God Complex*), Slagelse: Thermidor.

Rinpoche, S. (2002) *The Tibetan Book of Living and Dying*, New York: HarperCollins Publishers.

Vestergaard, A. (2000): 'Ekstremt: Den store nedtur' (Extreme: The Big Down), *Politiken*, Copenhagen: 20 February.

Index